Primary Source Readings in
Christian Morality

Primary Source Readings in
Christian Morality

Thaddeus Ostrowski
Robert Smith, FSC, PhD, general editor

saint mary's press

The publishing team included Steven C. McGlaun, development editor; Lorraine Kilmartin, reviewer; prepress and manufacturing coordinated by the production departments of Saint Mary's Press.

Konstantin Andy / Shutterstock, cover photo

Printed in the United States of America

1350

ISBN 978-0-88489-989-1

Library of Congress Cataloging-in-Publication Data

Ostrowski, Thaddeus.
    Primary source readings in Christian morality / Thaddeus Ostrowski ; Robert Smith, general editor.
        p. cm.
    Includes bibliographical references.
    ISBN 978-0-88489-989-1 (pbk.)
        1. Ten commandments—Juvenile literature. 2. Christian ethics—Catholic authors—Juvenile literature. 3. Catholic Church—Doctrines. I. Smith, Robert J., 1954– II. Title.

BV4656.O88 2008
241'.042—dc22

                                                    2007038237

Contents

Thaddeus Ostrowski holds a master of theological studies (MTS) degree from Vanderbilt Divinity School and is completing his doctoral work in moral theology at Boston College. While at Boston College, Thaddeus taught biblical heritage, and personal and social responsibility. He also spent two years in Rome as a teaching assistant and chaperone for Contemporary Catholic Ethics, a summer course for undergraduates, and worked with the Faith, Peace, and Justice Program for three years as a leader on a service-immersion trip to the Navajo Nation in New Mexico and Arizona.

Robert Smith, FSC, PhD, has been a De La Salle Christian Brother for the past thirty years. In that time he has held various positions, including vice president for mission, director of faculty development, and chair of the theology department at Saint Mary's University of Minnesota. He also spent three years as the dean and director of the Saint Mary's University Nairobi campus, in Kenya. In August 2007, he became the vice president for academic affairs at Bethlehem University in the West Bank, Palestine. Br. Robert Smith holds a PhD in moral theology from Marquette University and is an internationally respected speaker and author.

Introduction

by Robert Smith, FSC, PhD

Even if you are too young to have seen the original 1940 Walt Disney animated film *Pinocchio,* most of us have heard the well-known if little-heeded advice that Jiminy Cricket offered Pinocchio: "Let your conscience be your guide."

Strange as it may seem, Jiminy's advice aligns with both the Western classical philosophical tradition and the teaching practice of the Catholic Church in matters concerning moral issues and ethical decisions. From Aristotle to Thomas Aquinas to the documents of the Second Vatican Council, we have been told to follow our conscience. In fact, Catholics have been taught that we *must* follow our conscience, for that is where God speaks to us in the silence of our inmost being (adapted from *Pastoral Constitution on the Church in the Modern World* [*Gaudium et Spes*], no. 16).

Ah! If only it were so easy! Following one's conscience, like so many things in life, is relatively easy in theory. However, when confronted with difficult, real-life, complicated moral decisions, coming to terms with a decision of conscience is not an easy task. Yet it is a responsibility that each of us must take on.

Those of us who come at moral decision making from a faith stance and within a community of believers are given a lot of assistance and guidance that helps to form our conscience. The Catholic Church's teaching is a bit more nuanced than Jiminy Cricket's straightforward advice. The Church clearly teaches that we must follow our conscience, but the Church is careful and insightful when it teaches that we must follow a *well-formed* conscience. You might then ask, how do I develop a well-formed conscience?

A crucial, and first, guideline is that we form our conscience for ourselves but not by ourselves alone. When all is said and done, we are each responsible for the decisions we make, both good and bad. However, before we make a final decision, we must "do our homework." Not to seek advice, not to do the necessary research, not to listen to the wisdom of others with greater experience, not to consult experts . . . all can lead to an ill-informed decision.

It is easy to believe that we know it all and that others—parents (especially!), teachers, authority figures, "the Church"—can't teach us anything. As we grow older and have gained more life experience, we realize how profoundly we all need the insights, wisdom, experience, support, and guidance of others in our lives, especially when we are facing major decisions that carry significant moral import.

There are many sources of moral knowledge and resources that can help us shape a well-formed conscience. Among these are personal and communal experience (sometimes referred to as the "sensus fidelium" or "sense of the faithful"), the sciences, academic scholarship, Scripture, and the collective wisdom of the Church's two-thousand-year Spirit-guided insights and teachings. Each of these sources and resources is important; however, for Catholics, when it comes to developing a well-formed conscience, the official teaching of the Church takes pride of place and has a privileged (which is not to say *only*) role to play in the formation of our conscience.

This book offers a variety of Church documents and articles that can help assist us in the formation of our moral conscience. It is structured around the Ten Commandments as its organizing principle. These commandments have served as the primary shapers of and foundational guidelines for the Judeo-Christian moral conscience for three millennia. The first two chapters provide an introduction to moral theology. The next ten chapters follow in order of the presentation of the Ten Commandments in the Books of Exodus and Deuteronomy. Each chapter begins with an excerpt from the *Catechism of the Catholic Church (CCC)* addressing the topic of the chapter. This is followed by a text from a pope, a bishop, a body of bishops, or a member of the clergy, and then an essay or article by a layperson. These texts, each of them and all of them collectively, reflect the wisdom tradition of the Church and its insights into the human person. Each chapter concludes with a writing from a member of the clergy or a layperson that helps us place the commandment into our everyday lives. Together these writings can serve as one source of assistance and guidance in the process of forming our moral conscience when we are faced with difficult decisions.

Let your conscience be your guide? Of course! Jiminy Cricket's advice was right! But let it be a well-formed conscience, informed and guided by the Church's teachings as well as the thoughtful reflections, experience, wisdom, and knowledge of others who help form the Body of Christ and contribute to the community's "sensus fidelium."

Starting with Love

Moral conscience[1], present at the heart of the person, enjoins him at the appropriate moment to do good and to avoid evil. It also judges particular choices, approving those that are good and denouncing those that are evil.[2] It bears witness to the authority of truth in reference to the supreme Good to which the human person is drawn, and it welcomes the commandments. When he listens to his conscience, the prudent man can hear God speaking. (CCC, no. 1777)

> **conscience**
> awareness of right and wrong and a sense of duty to do the good

Introduction

When Angelo Guiseppe Roncalli was elected as the 261st pope of the Roman Catholic Church at the age of seventy-six on October 28, 1958, and took the name John XXIII, few anticipated the impact he would have on the Church. Due to his age, many assumed his papacy would be short and uneventful. Pope John XXIII indeed passed away fewer than five years after his election, but not before he called for the Second Vatican Council, also known as Vatican Council II. The Second Vatican Council, as one account goes, "threw open the windows of the Church so that we can see out and the people can see in." The times were changing, and so, it seems, was the Church.

Today the meaning of the Second Vatican Council and the changes it introduced are still under debate, but its legacy is felt every Sunday when Mass is celebrated in the common language of the community rather than in Latin, and in every classroom where moral theology is taught. The council was guided by the complementary trends of *aggiornamento,* which means "bringing up to date," and *ressourcement,* a desire to recover authentic traditions from the Church's past. Nowhere are these complementary movements more evident than in *Pastoral Constitution on the Church in the Modern World (Gaudium et Spes).* Promulgated by John XXIII's successor, Paul VI, on December 7, 1965, the document declares, "the Church has always had the duty of scrutinizing the signs of the times and of interpreting them in the light of the Gospel" (*The Church in the Modern World,* no. 4). By "opening the windows," John XXIII had asked the Church to read "the signs of the times," to draw on the vast resources of its traditions *(ressourcement),* and to speak the good news in a way relevant and meaningful to people today *(aggiornamento).* As a result, the Church asserted in the opening line (from which the document takes its name, *Gaudium et Spes,* meaning "joy and hope") that it shares the joys and hopes, the griefs and anxieties of all people.

But who—and what—are these people? *The Church in the Modern World* makes an invaluable contribution to moral theology by exploring the nature and dignity of the human person amidst the confusions and contradictions of the present day. Turning to Scripture, the document states that human beings have an inherent dignity because they are created in the image of God, that they are social beings who find fulfillment in community, and that people are weighed down and wounded by the power of sin. Despite the power of sin, human beings are blessed with freedom, conscience, and the intellect to seek truth.

> **freedom**
> the ability to respond to God's invitation to love and do the good

Many find in Vatican Council II a spirit of optimism and openness, particularly in its stirring description of the conscience.

Perhaps it is this optimism that emboldened James F. Keenan, SJ, who writes that he begins his courses on moral theology with the topic of love. For him, starting with love is one more way to "open the windows," draw on the sources of Scripture and tradition, and relate them to human experiences. Together, the council's teaching on the true freedom of the human person and Keenan's reflections on love begin our exploration of moral theology and the human person.

Excerpts from *Pastoral Constitution on the Church in the Modern World (Gaudium et Spes)*

by the Second Vatican Council

Chapter I

The Dignity of the Human Person

12. According to the almost unanimous opinion of believers and unbelievers alike, all things on earth should be related to man as their center and crown.

But what is man? About himself he has expressed, and continues to express, many divergent and even contradictory opinions. In these he often exalts himself as the absolute measure of all things or debases himself to the point of despair. The result is doubt and anxiety. The Church certainly understands these problems. Endowed with light from God, she can offer solutions to them, so that man's true situation can be portrayed and his defects explained, while at the same time his dignity and destiny are justly acknowledged.

For Sacred Scripture teaches that man was created "to the image of God," is capable of knowing and loving his Creator, and was appointed by Him as master of all earthly creatures that he might subdue them and use them to God's glory. "What is man that you should care for him? You have made him little less than the angels, and crowned him with glory and honor. You have given him rule over the works of your hands, putting all things under his feet" (Ps. 8:5–7).

But God did not create man as a solitary, for from the beginning "male and female he created them" (Gen. 1:27). Their companionship produces the primary form of interpersonal communion. For by his innermost nature man is a social being, and unless he relates himself to others he can neither live nor develop his potential.

liberty
the ability to make rational choices without external constraint

Therefore, as we read elsewhere in Holy Scripture God saw "all that he had made, and it was very good" (Gen. 1:31).

13. Although he was made by God in a state of holiness, from the very onset of his history man abused his liberty, at the urging of the Evil One. Man set himself against God and sought to attain his goal apart from God. Although they knew God, they did not glorify Him as God, but their senseless minds were darkened and they served the creature rather than the Creator. What divine revelation makes known to us agrees with experience. Examining his heart, man finds that he has inclinations toward evil too, and is engulfed by manifold ills which cannot come from his good Creator. Often refusing to acknowledge God as his

divine revelation
truths God has made known to humans, definitively revealed through Scripture and Sacred Tradition

beginning, man has disrupted also his proper relationship to his own ultimate goal as well as his whole relationship toward himself and others and all created things.

Therefore man is split within himself. As a result, all of human life, whether individual or collective, shows itself to be a dramatic struggle between good and evil, between light and darkness. Indeed, man finds that by himself he is incapable of battling the assaults of evil successfully, so that everyone feels as though he is bound by chains. But the Lord Himself came to free and strengthen man, renewing him inwardly and casting out that "prince of this world" (John 12:31) who held him in the bondage of sin. For sin has diminished man, blocking his path to fulfillment.

The call to grandeur and the depths of misery, both of which are a part of human experience, find their ultimate and simultaneous explanation in the light of this revelation.

14. Though made of body and soul, man is one. Through his bodily composition he gathers to himself the elements of the material world; thus they reach their crown through him, and through him raise their voice in free praise of the Creator. For this reason man is not allowed to despise his bodily life, rather he is obliged to regard his body as good and honorable since God has created it and will raise it up on the last day. Nevertheless, wounded by sin, man experiences rebellious stirrings in his body. But the very dignity of man postulates that man glorify God in his body and forbid it to serve the evil inclinations of his heart.

Now, man is not wrong when he regards himself as superior to bodily concerns, and as more than a speck of nature or a nameless constituent of the city of man. For by his interior qualities he outstrips the whole sum of mere things. He plunges into the depths of reality whenever he enters into his own heart; God, Who probes the heart, awaits him there; there he discerns his proper destiny beneath the eyes of God. Thus, when he recognizes in himself a spiritual and immortal soul, he is not being mocked by a fantasy born only of physical or social influences, but is rather laying hold of the proper truth of the matter.

15. Man judges rightly that by his intellect he surpasses the material universe, for he shares in the light of the divine mind. By relentlessly employing his talents through the ages he has indeed made progress in the practical sciences and in technology and the liberal arts. In our times he has won superlative victories, especially in his probing of the material world and in subjecting it to himself. Still he has always searched for more penetrating truths, and finds them. For his intelligence is not confined to observable data alone, but can with genuine certitude attain to reality itself as knowable, though in consequence of sin that certitude is partly obscured and weakened.

The intellectual nature of the human person is perfected by wisdom and needs to be, for wisdom gently attracts the mind of man to a quest and a love for what is true and good. Steeped in wisdom, man passes through visible realities to those which are unseen.

Our era needs such wisdom more than bygone ages if the discoveries made by man are to be further humanized. For the future of the world stands in peril unless wiser men are forthcoming. It should also be pointed out that many nations, poorer in economic goods, are quite rich in wisdom and can offer noteworthy advantages to others.

It is, finally, through the gift of the Holy Spirit that man comes by faith to the contemplation and appreciation of the divine plan.

16. In the depths of his conscience, man detects a law which he does not impose upon himself, but which holds him to obedience. Always summoning him to love good and avoid evil, the voice of conscience when necessary speaks to his heart: do this, shun that. For man has in his heart a law written by God; to obey it is the very dignity of man; according to it he will be judged. Conscience is the most secret core and sanctuary of a man. There he is alone with God, Whose voice echoes in his depths. In a wonderful manner conscience reveals that law which is fulfilled by love of God and neighbor. In fidelity to conscience, Christians are joined with the rest of men in the search for truth, and for the genuine solution to the numerous problems which arise in the life of individuals from social relationships. Hence the more right conscience holds sway, the more persons and groups turn aside from blind choice and strive to be guided by the objective norms of morality. Conscience frequently errs from invincible ignorance without losing its dignity. The same cannot be said for a man who cares but little for

license

a disregard for principles of personal conduct and moral laws truth and goodness, or for a conscience which by degrees grows practically sightless as a result of habitual sin.

17. Only in freedom can man direct himself toward goodness. Our contemporaries make much of this freedom and pursue it eagerly; and rightly to be sure. Often however they foster it perversely as a license for doing whatever pleases them, even if it is evil. For its part, authentic freedom is an exceptional sign of the divine image within man. For God has willed that man remain "under the control of his own decisions," so that he can seek his Creator spontaneously, and come freely to utter and blissful perfection through loyalty to Him. Hence man's dignity demands that he act according to a knowing and free choice that is personally motivated and prompted from within, not under blind internal impulse nor by mere external pressure. Man achieves such dignity when, emancipating himself from all captivity to passion, he pursues his goal in a spontaneous choice of what is good, and procures for himself through effective and skilful action, apt helps to that end. Since man's freedom has been damaged by sin, only by the aid of God's grace can he bring such a relationship with God into full flower. Before the judgment seat of God each man must render an account of his own life, whether he has done good or evil.

18. It is in the face of death that the riddle of human existence grows most acute. Not only is man tormented by pain and by the advancing deterioration of his body, but even more so by a dread of perpetual extinction. He rightly follows the intuition of his heart when he abhors and repudiates the utter ruin and total disappearance of his own person. He rebels against death because he bears

in himself an eternal seed which cannot be reduced to sheer matter. All the endeavors of technology, though useful in the extreme, cannot calm his anxiety; for prolongation of biological life is unable to satisfy that desire for higher life which is inescapably lodged in his breast.

Although the mystery of death utterly beggars the imagination, the Church has been taught by divine revelation and firmly teaches that man has been created by God for a blissful purpose beyond the reach of earthly misery. In addition, that bodily death from which man would have been immune had he not sinned will be vanquished, according to the Christian faith, when man who was ruined by his own doing is restored to wholeness by an almighty and merciful Saviour. For God has called man and still calls him so that with his entire being he might be joined to Him in an endless sharing of a divine life beyond all corruption. Christ won this victory when He rose to life, for by His death He freed man from death. Hence to every thoughtful man a solidly established faith provides the answer to his anxiety about what the future holds for him. At the same time faith gives him the power to be united in Christ with his loved ones who have already been snatched away by death; faith arouses the hope that they have found true life with God.

Excerpt from *Moral Wisdom: Lessons and Texts from the Catholic Tradition*

by James F. Keenan, SJ

Starting with Love

I teach an introductory course on moral theology, and during my fifteen years teaching it, I only recently learned to begin my course on the topic of love. Not only did I not begin with love, I never even taught a class on it.

For me love was what the philosophers call "formal." God loves us; we love God; we are called to morality as a response to that love, so let's discuss morality. Admittedly, like all Christians I acknowledged that love has always been the foundation of my life and, in particular, my ethical vision. I also recognized that love was charity and that charity moved us. But I took it all for granted.

> **formal**
> merely logical; independent of (or prior to) specific experience

I began my course on freedom, a freedom for God, church, and neighbor. My mentor, Josef Fuchs, always started with freedom. He called this a basic freedom, a freedom in grace to realize the call of Christ. Others like Pope John Paul II and Cardinal Josef Ratzinger usually begin their writings on ethics with truth. They talk about the

> **charity**
> God's love of humans, which through the indwelling of the Holy Spirit causes humans to love God and neighbor

need to base all ethics on truth. In many ways the tension between moral theologians and teachers of the moral magisterium has been the preference each side has for either freedom or truth.

But now I believe we need to start with the primacy of love and specifically the love of God. Why love?

If we start with love instead of freedom or truth, what happens? Why start discussions of morality and ethics with love? Let me give you three reasons—from the scriptures, theology, and the tradition rooted in human experience—for starting with the love of God.

First, the scriptures command it. Not only does Jesus teach us that the love of God is the first command, but the Ten Commandments themselves recognize the love and honor for God as the first commandment of all. On it depend all the other commandments. Knowing that the commandments were not imposed on us for God's pleasure, but rather for our benefit and our flourishment, by insisting on God's sovereignty, the first commandment makes our dependency on God the very foundation of our happiness.

> **temporal**
> pertaining to physical existence in time

> **flourishment**
> growth into full and healthy humanity

Second, the love of God precedes whatever else we discuss in theology, whether we speak temporally or metaphysically. For instance, love is how we understand God, for God is love. Karl Rahner tells us that because

God is love, God is triune, for God needs to be in God's self more than one person in order to be love, for the lover needs the beloved. Love also explains the creation. Again,

> **triune**
> three in one; adjective referring to the three persons in one God

Rahner tells us that because God is love, God "needs" to love more than God's self. For that reason God creates us so as to enter into love with us, to bring us into God's kingdom. Love also is the ground of our redemption, for "God so loved the world that God gave God's one and only Son, that whoever believes in him shall not perish but have eternal life" (John 3:16). Love, too, is the way of our sanctification, for Jesus commanded us to love God, to love our neighbor, and to love ourselves. Finally, love is our goal, for in the kingdom we believe that we will be united forever with God and those who have gone before us. Thus, love is our understanding of God, creation, redemption, sanctification,

> **metaphysical**
> pertaining to the essence of things beyond what can be perceived by the five senses

> **sanctification**
> being made holy or pure; growth in holiness

> **redemption**
> delivery from sin; atonement for guilt

and eschatological promise: In as much as theology is the study of God, then love is the beginning and end of theology, for God is love.

Listen to how the first Letter of John comprehensively presents it:

> [7]Dear friends, let us love one another, for love comes from God. Everyone who loves has been born of God and knows God. [8]Whoever does not love does not know God, because God is love. [9]This is how God showed God's love among us: God sent God's one and only Son into the world that we might live through him. [10]This is love: not that we loved God, but that God loved us and sent his Son as an atoning sacrifice for our sins. [11]Dear friends, since God so loved us, we also ought to love one another.

> [16]God is love. Whoever lives in love lives in God, and God in them. [17]In this way, love is made complete among us so that we will have confidence on the day of judgment, because in this world we are like God.

> [19]We love because God first loved us. [20]If anyone says, "I love God," yet hates one's brother or sister, that one is a liar. For anyone who does not love one's brother or sister, whom we have seen, cannot love God, whom we have not seen. [21]And God has given us this command: Whoever loves God must also love their brother and sister. (1 John 7–11, 16–17, 19–21)

A third reason for beginning with the love of God is that human experience confirms that unlike freedom or truth, love drives, animates, moves. It is what prompted the cell phone calls on September 11, 2001, the handing over of the human spirit looking for union. Not only does love look for union, it also moves us toward freedom and truth. Love then makes possible our search for a freedom for greater love and a truth to love rightly.

One of the most important works in moral theology in the twentieth century specifically turned to the tradition to confirm this truth from human experience. In *The Primacy of Charity in Moral Theology*, Gérard Gilleman insists that we need an experience-based moral theology that starts at the depths of our being. He turned to charity, the love of God dwelling in us, and there he tapped into the notion of spiritual or devotional theology nourishing the depths of our spirit. When we think of charity, Gilleman quoted Thomas Aquinas as saying, we must realize that the love of God is no less than the presence of the Holy Spirit in us. Herein we find the love of God, charity animating us. Gilleman also invokes Thomas calling charity the mother of the virtues, again because it precedes all other virtues by animating them and giving them life.

Tradition constantly confirms this human experience of the love of God preceding all else. For instance, our tradition testifies, time and again, to the love of God as the foundation of the call to become a Christian. Of course, the paradigmatic conversion marked by love is Augustine's (354–430) own. Augustine, who converted to Christianity in his early thirties, insisted on the primacy of love—"Love and do as you will." He describes in the tenth book of the *Confessions* the deeply felt, passionate, visceral pursuit of the love of God:

Late it was that I loved you, beauty so ancient and so new, late I loved you! And, look, you were within me and I was outside, and there I sought for you and in my ugliness I plunged into the beauties that you have made. You were with me and I was not with you. Those outer beauties kept me far from you, yet if they had not been in you, they would not have existed at all. You called, you cried out, you shattered my deafness: you flashed, you shone, you scattered my blindness: you breathed perfume, and I drew in my breath and I pant for you: I tasted, and I am hungry and thirsty: you touched me, and I burned for your peace.

Augustine's conversion was a response to the love of God already within him. Similarly, the conversion of St. Paul, who also testified to the primacy of love, was a call of love. Of course, unlike Augustine, we do not have from Paul the description of his conversion in quite the poetry that Augustine provided, but for the great evangelizer who wanted nothing but Christ, certainly he understood Christ's call as nothing but love.

I first came to this insight not from the Letters of Paul—though it was always there—but in a painting by Caravaggio (1573–1610). To appreciate Caravaggio's painting, I want to compare it with an earlier one by Michelangelo (1475–1564).

In Michelangelo's *Conversion of St. Paul* (1542–1545), God, accompanied by angels and saints, erupts from heaven and parts the sky, allowing heaven's light to aim tornado-like on the person of Paul. God intervenes directly onto a plain, sending Paul's horse and at least fifteen soldiers away in flight. In the lower left-hand corner of the canvas, an elder, white-bearded, stunned Paul shields his face as he turns toward the light with his companion helping him to his feet. The painting is clearly about the power of God entering dramatically and definitively into human history.

In Caravaggio's *Conversion of Paul* (1600), there are only three figures, Paul, his horse, and Paul's companion tending to the horse. On a fairly dark background we see Paul young, in vibrant passionate colors of orange, red, blue, and yellow, wearing armor, very handsome on his back, legs opened, eyes closed. The conversion is an ecstatic moment in which Paul is purely recipient of God's love. It has a deeply erotic tone. The horse and his companion do not flee but remain standing there, neither aware of what is happening to Paul. Only Paul in his deep interiority is receiving the Lord. He is in union with the Lord. This deep, internalized conversion clearly conveys that God is doing something to Paul.

In this painting, unlike Michelangelo's, God is not visible. God is present, nonetheless, but in Paul, because someone is doing something to Paul. Caravaggio captures Paul's experience, making sure that the agent we see active is not Paul but God. Thus, even though you see God in Michelangelo's, still your eyes move to Paul. In Caravaggio's, you see Paul, but you look for God.

This move by Caravaggio is insightful. The event is not Paul being turned around. The event is Paul becoming deeply attuned to the presence of the love of God in his life. Of course, only one who has known that experience could insist that love is the only thing that lasts.

The greatness of our tradition is that the love of God is not simply the beginning of the Christian's life but the whole continuum of it. Thus, in the Church of Maria del Popolo, Caravaggio's *Conversion of Paul* hangs in front of his *Crucifixion of Peter*. Like Paul, Peter is on his back, but his back is on a cross, and while the stimulated Paul is completely clothed, the aging flesh of Peter is fairly exposed, but hardly erotic. Peter is looking at his hands, fastened to the cross. He inevitably recalls the questioning on the beach—"Do you love me?"—and the prediction that Peter, when he is old, shall stretch forth his hands and be led where he will not want to go (John 21:15–19).

In two paintings, Caravaggio captures the beginning and the end of the Christian life as a life living out of the love of God.

For Reflection

1. When you hear the term *morality*, what do you think of? In what ways do these two readings present an understanding of Christian morality that is similar to or different from the view you have? Explain.

2. According to *The Church in the Modern World,* what is the purpose of freedom? Provide examples from the reading supporting your answer. How does this view of freedom coincide with and differ from the view of freedom presented in our society?

3. Why does James Keenan, SJ, in *Moral Wisdom: Lessons and Texts from the Catholic Tradition,* decide to start with love rather than freedom in presenting Christian morality? Provide an explanation citing the reading.

4. In a library or online, find a copy of Carvaggio's *Conversion of Paul* and Michelangelo's *Conversion of St. Paul.* Write a paragraph explaining which one best matches your experience of God.

Endnotes

1. Cf. *Rom* 2:14–16.
2. Cf. *Rom* 1:32.

Understanding Truth and Sin

By his reason, man recognizes the voice of God which urges him "to do what is good and avoid what is evil."[1] Everyone is obliged to follow this law, which makes itself heard in conscience and is fulfilled in the love of God and of neighbor. Living a moral life bears witness to the dignity of the person. (*CCC*, no. 1706)

Introduction

The Splendor of Truth (*Veritatis Splendor*), promulgated by Pope John Paul II on August 6, 1993, is the Church's most recent and comprehensive statement on moral theology. Appearing after the collapse of both the wall dividing East and West Berlin and Communism in the Soviet Union, *The Splendor of Truth* addressed a threat less tangible but perhaps more pervasive than Communism: moral relativism. Moral relativism is the position that there are no universal truths and objective moral standards, only different opinions. Its influence is everywhere, from ethical debates between friends ("Well, that is fine for you, but it is not what I believe.") to discussions about the legitimacy of laws ("Who can say what is right? Everyone has to decide for herself.").

The Splendor of Truth contrasts this moral relativism with truth. All human beings, it asserts, instinctively search for truth and meaning, which is found in the revelation of Jesus Christ, who is "the way, the truth, and the life" (John 14:6). We are gifted with freedom and conscience for the sake of discovering and living the truth. Freedom, from the Catholic perspective, is not license to do whatever one wants, but the gift and ability to choose the good; conscience is not merely the latitude to decide what one feels, but the power to determine what is truly right. The teaching of the Magisterium, through its interpretation of Scripture and Tradition, helps inform our freedom and conscience.

While *The Splendor of Truth* is best known for its unflinching assertion that some acts are always and everywhere wrong and therefore forbidden, it situates this claim within an understanding that a moral life is a response to Jesus's invitation "Come, follow me." The following excerpt, taken from the first chapter of *The Splendor of Truth*, is a meditation on the story of the rich young man from Saint Matthew's Gospel (19:16–21). It portrays the moral life as a pilgrimage characterized not by the burden of obeying rules, but by the joy and fulfillment that comes with being a disciple of the Lord. While affirming that the Ten Commandments remain valid

obligation
a duty

obligations, *The Splendor of Truth* invites us to recognize the duty to love God and neighbor as a way of returning the love God first showed for us.

Moral theology underwent an important change in the twentieth century. For a long time it was shaped by the practice of the sacrament of Penance and Reconciliation; penitents had to avoid or confess sins and receive forgiveness so they could go to heaven. But *The Splendor of Truth* illustrates a shift in thinking. The rich young man said he had kept the commandments, yet asked what he still lacked. Likewise, moral theology has begun to focus not just on avoiding evil, but increasingly on *doing good*. What happens to the concept of sin when such a shift occurs?

In the second reading, Richard M. Gula, SS, offers an account of these developments and presents a vivid understanding of sin today. He explains that a relational model of the moral life, in which responsibility is the key characteristic, has supplanted the legalistic model wherein sin is akin to a crime. Gula then elaborates on the meaning of familiar types of sin—original, social, mortal, and venial—in this new framework. He concludes by reminding us that any serious assessment of sin leads us to a profound recognition of God's mercy.

Excerpt from *The Splendor of Truth (Veritatis Splendor)*

by Pope John Paul II

Chapter I–"Teacher, What Good Must I Do . . . ?" *(Mt 19:16)*–**Christ and the answer to the question about morality**

"Someone came to him . . . " (*Mt* 19:16)

6. *The dialogue of Jesus with the rich young man,* related in the nineteenth chapter of Saint Matthew's Gospel, can serve as a useful guide *for listening once more* in a lively and direct way to his moral teaching: "Then someone came to him and said, 'Teacher, what good must I do to have eternal life?' And he said to him, 'Why do you ask me about what is good? There is only one who is good. If you wish to enter into life, keep the commandments.' He said to him, 'Which ones?' And Jesus said, 'You shall not murder; You shall not commit adultery; You shall not steal; You shall not bear false witness; Honour your father and mother; also, You shall love your neighbour as yourself.' The young man said to him, 'I have kept all these; what do I still lack?' Jesus said to him, 'If you wish to be perfect, go, sell your possessions and give the money to the poor, and you will have treasure in heaven; then come, follow me'" (*Mt* 19:16–21).

7. *"Then someone came to him . . ."* In the young man, whom Matthew's Gospel does not name, we can recognize every person who, consciously or not, *approaches Christ the Redeemer of man and questions him about morality.* For the young man, the *question* is not so much about rules to be followed, but *about the full meaning of life.* This is in fact the aspiration at the heart of every human decision and action, the quiet searching and interior prompting which sets freedom in motion. This question is ultimately an appeal to the absolute Good which attracts us and beckons us; it is the echo of a call from God who is the origin and goal of man's life.

vocation

a calling to serve God; purpose in life

Church

the people of God; followers of Jesus across time and space

Precisely in this perspective the Second Vatican Council called for a renewal of moral theology, so that its teaching would display the lofty vocation which the faithful have received in Christ, the only response fully capable of satisfying the desire of the human heart.

In order to make this "encounter" with Christ possible, God willed his Church. Indeed, the Church "wishes to serve this single end: that each person may be able to find Christ, in order that Christ may walk with each person the path of life."

"Teacher, what good must I do to have eternal life?" (Mt 19:16)

8. The question which the rich young man puts to Jesus of Nazareth is one which rises from the depths of his heart. It is *an essential and unavoidable question for the life of every man,* for it is about the moral good which must be done, and about eternal life. The young man senses that there is a connection between moral good and the fulfilment of his own destiny. He is a devout Israelite, raised as it were in the shadow of the Law of the Lord. If he asks Jesus this question, we can presume that it is not because he is ignorant of the answer contained in the Law. It is more likely that the attractiveness of the person of Jesus had prompted within him new questions about moral good. He feels the need to draw near to the One who had

begun his preaching with this new and decisive proclamation: "The time is fulfilled, and the Kingdom of God is
at hand; repent, and believe in the Gospel" (*Mk* 1:15).

*People today need to turn to Christ once again in
order to receive from him the answer to their questions
about what is good and what is evil.* Christ is the Teacher,
the Risen One who has life in himself and who is always
present in his Church and in the world. It is he who opens
up to the faithful the book of the Scriptures and, by fully
revealing the Father's will, teaches the truth about moral
action. At the source and summit of the economy of
salvation, as the Alpha and the Omega of human history
(cf. *Rev* 1:8; 21:6; 22:13), Christ sheds light on man's
condition and his integral vocation. Consequently, "the
man who wishes to understand himself thoroughly—and
not just in accordance with immediate, partial, often
superficial, and even illusory standards and measures of
his being—must with his unrest, uncertainty and even his
weakness and sinfulness, with his life and death, draw
near to Christ. He must, so to speak, enter him with all his
own self; he must 'appropriate' and assimilate the whole
of the reality of the Incarnation and Redemption in order
to find himself. If this profound process takes place within
him, he then bears fruit not only of adoration of God but
also of deeper wonder at himself."

If we therefore wish to go to the heart of the Gospel's
moral teaching and grasp its profound and unchanging
content, we must carefully inquire into the meaning of
the question asked by the rich young man in the Gospel
and, even more, the meaning of Jesus' reply, allowing
ourselves to be guided by him. Jesus, as a patient and

sensitive teacher, answers the young man by taking him, as it were, by the hand, and leading him step by step to the full truth.

"There is only one who is good" (Mt 19:17)

9. Jesus says: "Why do you ask me about what is good? There is only one who is good. If you wish to enter into life, keep the commandments" (*Mt* 19:17). In the versions of the Evangelists Mark and Luke the question is phrased in this way: "Why do you call me good? No one is good but God alone" (*Mk* 10:18; cf. *Lk* 18:19).

Before answering the question, Jesus wishes the young man to have a clear idea of why he asked his question. The "Good Teacher" points out to him —and to all of us—that the answer to the question, "What good must I do to have eternal life?" can only be found by turning one's mind and heart to the "One" who is good: "No one is good but God alone" (*Mk* 10:18; cf. *Lk* 18:19). *Only God can answer the question about what is good, because he is the Good itself.*

To ask about the good, in fact, *ultimately means to turn towards God,* the fullness of goodness. Jesus shows that the young man's question is really a *religious question,* and that the goodness that attracts and at the same time obliges man has its source in God, and indeed is God himself. God alone is worthy of being loved "with all one's heart, and with all one's soul, and with all one's mind" (*Mt* 22:37). He is the source of man's happiness. Jesus brings the question about morally good action back to its religious foundations, to the acknowledgment of

God, who alone is goodness, fullness of life, the final end of human activity, and perfect happiness.

10. The Church, instructed by the Teacher's words, believes that man, made in the image of the Creator, redeemed by the Blood of Christ and made holy by the presence of the Holy Spirit, has as the *ultimate purpose of his life to live "for the praise of God's glory"* (cf. *Eph* 1:12), striving to make each of his actions reflect the splendour of that glory. "Know, then, O beautiful soul, that you are *the image of God,"* writes Saint Ambrose. "Know that you are *the glory of God* (*1 Cor* 11:7). Hear how you are his glory. The Prophet says: *Your knowledge has become too wonderful for me* (cf. *Ps.* 138:6, Vulg.). That is to say, in my work your majesty has become more wonderful; in the counsels of men your wisdom is exalted. When I consider myself, such as I am known to you in my secret thoughts and deepest emotions, the mysteries of your knowledge are disclosed to me. Know then, O man, your greatness, and be vigilant."

What man is and what he must do becomes clear as soon as God reveals himself. The Decalogue is based on these words: "I am the Lord your God, who brought you out of the land of Egypt, out of the house of bondage" (*Ex* 20:2–3). In the "ten words" of the Covenant with Israel, and in the whole Law, God makes himself known and acknowledged as the One who " alone is good"; the One who despite man's sin remains the "model" for moral action, in accordance with his

> **Decalogue**
> meaning "ten words"; another name for the Ten Commandments

command, "You shall be holy; for I the Lord your God am holy" (*Lev* 19:2); as the One who, faithful to his love for man, gives him his Law (cf. *Ex* 19:9–24 and 20:18–21) in order to restore man's original and peaceful harmony with the Creator and with all creation, and, what is more, to draw him into his divine love: "I will walk among you, and will be your God, and you shall be my people" (*Lev* 26:12).

The moral life presents itself as the response due to the many gratuitous initiatives taken by God out of love for man. It is a response of love, according to the statement made in Deuteronomy about the fundamental commandment: "Hear, O Israel: The Lord our God is one Lord; and you shall love the Lord your God with all your heart, and with all your soul, and with all your might. And these words which I command you this day shall be upon your heart; and you shall teach them diligently to your children" (*Dt* 6:4–7). Thus the moral life, caught up in the gratuitousness of God's love, is called to reflect his glory: "For the one who loves God it is enough to be pleasing to the One whom he loves: for no greater reward should be sought than that love itself; charity in fact is of God in such a way that God himself is charity."

Excerpts from "Understanding Sin Today"

by Richard M. Gula, SS

"Bless me, Father, for I have sinned. It has been six weeks since my last confession. I lost my patience three times; I lied twice; I missed Mass once; I had impure thoughts twice and I gossiped about my neighbor four times."

Sound familiar? The above confession reflects an understanding of the moral life and sin that prevailed among Roman Catholics for centuries. But in the last half of this century, many changes have been occurring in the way we think about morality and sin. These changes have resulted in part from new ways of understanding what it means to be human. They also come from rediscovering old ideas that the Bible and Jesus taught about how we ought to relate to God and to one another.

Sin as crime

There was a time when Catholics thought that living morally was mostly a matter of obeying the law—the divine law or the commandments of God, the ecclesial (Church) laws or the natural laws expressed in the moral teaching of the Church. "It's in the Bible" or "The Church says so" were often our most important reasons for being moral.

Sin was like a crime, a transgression of the law. It was akin to breaking the speed limit on the highway. The law is what made an action sinful. Where there was no clear-cut law (no speed limit), there was no question of sin (go as fast as you want).

Catholic theology has since come to realize that the legal model for understanding the moral life and sin is deficient. For one thing, the demands of being a faithful follower of Jesus, of living according to the vision and values of the gospel, stretch us farther than what can be prescribed by law.

But no one is trying to do away with laws. We know that laws will always be necessary to help us live together well. Just as our city streets would be chaos without traffic laws, so our living together would be a moral chaos without laws like those about telling the truth, respecting property and protecting life.

But laws cannot possibly cover all the decisions that we have to make. The legal model of the moral life too easily makes moral living a matter of repeating the same old behaviors even though we—and our world—have changed. The legal model also tends to focus too much on the actions that we do as being sinful or not. Did I miss Mass? Did I cheat on an exam or on my taxes? Did I disobey my parents?

Laws by themselves don't address the important realities of the heart, such as our attitudes (Are we kind or hostile?), intentions (Do we strive to be helpful or self-serving?) and ways of seeing things (Do we look through the eyes of faith? Are we optimistic or pessimistic?). Jesus reminds us that what comes from the heart is what makes one sinful. Sinful actions are like the tip of an iceberg being held above the surface by a wayward heart (see Is 29:13; Mk 7:21; Mt 23:25–26; Lk 6:45).

The legal model also tends to make the moral life too centered on one's self. Sin affects me and my salvation. Saving my soul through obedience is the guiding moral principle according to this model. This leaves out, however, the all-important relational dimensions of sin and conversion. As St. Paul teaches, no one lives for oneself (Rom 14:7). As the Body of Christ, we suffer together and rejoice together (1 Cor

> **conversion**
> a change of heart with the intention of following God more faithfully

12:26–27). Because we share a common world, we are part of a network of relationships that joins each of us in responsibility to others and to all of creation. We all know that we violate the ecological balance of nature when we put toxins into our air and water or throw hamburger foil wrappers out the car window. We violate our moral ecology when we create discord, dissension, fear, mistrust and alienation in the web of life's relationships.

Sin's new look

A new look at the moral life has been informed by the biblical renewal in the Church and by some philosophical shifts within the Church and society.

For example, the biblical renewal has given us covenant, heart and conversion—not law—as our primary moral concepts. Responsibility has replaced obligation as the primary characteristic of the moral life. Shifts in philosophy have emphasized the dignity of persons and the value of sharing life in society. Together these shifts in theology and philosophy support a *relational* model of the moral life. The relational model emphasizes personal responsibility for protecting the bonds of peace and justice that sustain human relationships.

What might a contemporary confession sound like that reflects the relational model of the moral life?

"Bless me, Father, for I have sinned. It has been six weeks since my last confession. I am a husband, a father of three teenage children, and I hold an executive position in a large computer firm.

"Over the past month I have allowed love to grow cold at home and in my work. At home, I have been inattentive to my wife and children as I allowed my new projects at work to consume most of my time and attention. I have spent more time at work and little time with the family. At work, I have selfishly neglected to disclose some data which my colleagues needed for a new project. I wanted to gain the glory. I have also failed to support a female colleague who was clearly being sexually harassed and I failed to confront those who were doing the harassing.

"I think a good penance for me, Father, would be to take the family on a picnic this week and to make a special effort to affirm my junior colleagues for the great work they have been doing."

This penitent senses how he is affecting the quality of life and love in his primary relationships. He also knows what he can do to show conversion. His confession reflects contemporary theology's emphasis on responsibility to others over the traditional overemphasis on what is allowed or forbidden by law. Rather than focusing just on committing sinful acts, it shows that sin is also an omission, a failure to do what ought to be done.

Far from doing away with sin, contemporary theology admits that sin is very much with us and touches us more deeply than we realize. Greed, violence, corruption, poverty, hunger, sexism and oppression are too prevalent to ignore.

Sin is just as basic a term in our Christian vocabulary today as it has been in the past. Its root sense means to be disconnected from God through the failure to love. In sin, we simply don't bother about anyone outside ourselves. Sin is first a matter of a selfish heart—a refusal to care— before it shows itself in actions. Because loving God and loving our neighbor are all tied together, sin will always be expressed in and through our relationships. . . .

My favorite example of how this relational vision of sin and the moral life influenced another's behavior came from my five-year-old niece, Julia. She listened to a conversation I was having with her eight-year-old sister about what she was being taught in her preparation for first Penance. The lesson on sin was filled with stories of relationships and the difference between loving and unloving choices. The next day, when Julia came home from kindergarten, I asked her how her day was. She said, "I had a good day." When I asked her what made it good, she said, "I had an opportunity to make a loving choice. Kenny forgot to bring a snack today, so I gave him one of my pretzels."

Julia learned quite well that right moral living begins with caring for one another: paying attention to another's needs and acting in a way that enhances another's well-being. Sin, by contrast, turns in and sets oneself against another. Self-serving interests destroy the bonds of peace and justice that ought to sustain us.

Original sin didn't go away

In an age when evils on a massive scale frequently make front-page news (wars, ethnic genocide, bombings, terrorism), theologians are trying to revive the doctrine of original sin. This doctrine tells us that there is more evil in the world than that which we cause ourselves. Consider the children being born in Rwanda or Bosnia today. They are affected and infected by the evil that surrounds them before they are ever able to make choices of their own.

Original sin is the face of sin which we recognize as the condition of evil into which we are all born. It is a condition of being human that makes us feel as if our freedom were bound by chains from the very beginning. We feel the effects of this evil in the pull towards selfishness which alienates us from our deeper selves, from others and from God. Because of original sin, we will always know struggle and tragedy as part of our life. . . .

Social sin—a life of its own

Social sin has been around as long as civilization, but it is a relatively new concept for Catholics. We have tended to focus exclusively on personal (actual) sin: lying, cheating, missing Mass. We have not paid sufficient attention to social structures and customs which hold such sinful practices in place. We are changing, however. One clear example of a rising social consciousness can be seen in Pope John Paul II's 1995 "Letter to Women." Here he publicly acknowledges sexism as a social sin and then goes on to apologize to women for the ways the Church has complied in denigrating women, misrepresenting them, reducing them to servitude and marginalizing them from society.

Social sin describes human-made structures when they offend human dignity by causing people to suffer oppression, exploitation or marginalization. These include educational systems, housing policies, tax structures, immigration policies, health-care systems, employment policies, a market economy. Once established, social structures and customs seem to take on a life of their own. The social sin of racism, for example, has continued and still continues long after slavery was abolished. For example, there remain obstacles to adequate education, to housing, to work, sometimes even to voting.

We learn to live in a world with these structures. We presume that the social customs which they hold in place are good, traditional customs. That is what makes social sin so difficult to recognize and to change. Yet the evil of sinful social structures abounds in all forms of discrimination, racism and sexism; in the exploitation of migrant workers; in the illiteracy and homelessness of the poor; in the lack of basic health care for all; in the manipulation of consumers by the manufacturing practices, advertising, pricing policies and packaging of goods; and in many other practices which we continue to support more out of ignorance than meanness. Why does social sin prevail? Largely because we fail to name social evils and seek to correct them. . . .

When we become aware of structural evils, we should not be paralyzed by the guilt of self-condemnation, but moved to conversion. Conversion from social sin involves, at one level, changing our own lifestyle in ways that will help reform society. We cannot do everything to end the structures which support sexism, for example, but we can do some things, for instance, curbing our use of exclusive and insensitive language. We can influence others' attitudes through the ways we talk to and about one another. At another level, conversion from social sin involves examining existing regulations and practices, reforming those that offend human dignity.

Actual sin—we all know it

Another face of sin is personal sin. Our traditional way of distinguishing the degrees of gravity of personal sins is to call them *mortal* and *venial* sins.

Catholics traditionally have been taught that for sin to be mortal, three conditions have to be met: 1) serious matter; 2) sufficient reflection; 3) full consent of the will.

These are still valuable criteria. They are comprehensive in including conditions which pertain to the action (1) and to the person (2 & 3) before we can speak of mortal sin in its truest sense.

The relational model of the moral life helps us to understand actual sin as primarily an expression of the person in relationship, not simply as disobedience to the law.

Mortal sin. Mortal sin is a serious break in a relationship of love with God, neighbor, world and self. We can think of it as a radical No to God and to others. It happens when we refuse to live in a positive, life-giving way. Just as acts of heroism and extraordinary generosity are evidence of our capacity to say a radical Yes to God, so calculated acts permeated with malice are evidence of our capacity to say No to God. Mortal sin involves a moral evil done by a person who is supremely selfish and committed to making evil and not goodness the characteristic mark of his or her life.

While we would not be surprised to find mortal sin in those who choose to make crime, extortion or greed a way of life, we must still be wary of judging another. No one can ever know for sure just by looking from the sidelines whether a particular act of malice is a mortal sin or not. We need to know more about the person's knowledge, freedom and fundamental disposition before God. We must refrain from judging others as being in mortal sin, even though we know their acts are permeated with evil. That is why the Church has never taught that anyone is, *in fact*, in hell. At the same time the Church acknowledges that we all have the *capacity* to cut ourselves off from the source of life that is God, which is a good description of hell.

Venial sin. These days people are not giving enough attention to immoral acts of less importance than mortal sin. If mortal sin radically reverses one's positive relationship to God, the habit of unloving acts can corrode that relationship. This is why we must take venial sins seriously. Venial sins can weigh us down with the anchor of bad habits.

Venial sin often enters our lives when we fail to show care for others. People can easily become submerged in self-interest. Perhaps we speak sharply to another, revel in our piece of gossip or exercise a power play over another that keeps us secure and in control. While these acts of selfish arrogance do not radically turn us away from God, they are inconsistent with our basic commitment to be for life and for love. They are venial sins.

Contemporary notions of sin emphasize the gospel's call to conversion in and through the web of life's relationships. The more clearly we can recognize God's presence and love in these relationships, the more clearly we can recognize our venial sins, and the more seriously we can take them. Without recognizing our sinfulness, we cannot grow in converting to the demands of love.

God is merciful

These are only some of the significant changes in our understanding of sin. We are talking about sin differently today because the relational model of the moral life has replaced the legal model. One thing that hasn't changed, though, is our concept of God's love and mercy. We do not believe that God wants us to be weighed down with a distorted sense of guilt and responsibility. Rather, we believe that we are called to participate more fully in the creative power of God calling us to reconciliation, to reconnect with our best selves, with others, with the world and with God.

The Sacrament of Penance and Reconciliation is an opportunity and invitation to heal the brokenness in our lives and to set relationships right. We should give more attention to celebrating this gift, especially during the seasons of Lent and Advent.

For Reflection

1. Explain how the moral life is "a response of love" as stated in *The Splendor of Truth*.

2. How is your understanding and experience of the sacrament of Penance and Reconciliation similar to the example provided at the beginning of "Understanding Sin Today"? What do you feel is the goal of the penance given in the example?

3. What are three social sins you encounter or witness in your life? What is a morally appropriate response by an individual to these social sins?

4. What does Richard Gula mean when he talks about conversion? Cite two examples from the selected reading. How is the conversion he speaks about similar to the message Jesus gives to the rich young man?

Endnotes

1. *Gaudium et spes* 16.

3

The First Commandment: "I am the LORD your God . . . you shall have no other gods before me."

Jesus summed up man's duties toward God in this saying: "You shall love the Lord your God with all your heart, and with all your soul, and with all your mind."[1] This immediately echoes the solemn call: "Hear, O Israel: the LORD our God is one LORD."[2] (*CCC*, no. 2083)

Introduction

We are not unlike the ancient Israelites in that a number of foreign gods compete for our allegiance. Money, fame, and nationalism are just a few of the many idols that tempt us today, and we are diminished when we let them shape the meaning of our lives. We are created in God's image, but we also can take on the reflection of our false deities. In which god we place our trust, therefore, is as important as whether we

idol
a false god

believe in any god at all. The first commandment clarifies this issue by specifying exactly which God we owe our exclusive worship to and the reason why. God is the liberator of the slaves in Egypt, just as God is the creator (Genesis) and redeemer (New Testament). God can neither be adequately represented nor replaced by the things of creation or the objects of human making.

The encyclical *God Is Love (Deus Caritas Est)* shares the first commandment's concern with God's identity and nature. Uncertainty and apprehension surrounded Benedict XVI's election as Pope. John Paul II's papacy had lasted twenty-six years, from 1978 to 2005, and Cardinal Josef Ratzinger (now Pope Benedict XVI) was associated so closely with him that many wondered how he would distinguish himself. In a previous reading, James Keenan noted the preference of John Paul II and Benedict XVI for the concept of truth over freedom. By choosing the topic of love for his first encyclical, Benedict XVI confounded expectations. The decision could not have been more appropriate, however, as the first commandment indicates that we know God through God's loving activity. Faithfulness to this God who is love, the one true God, has profound ramifications for our lives. In the following selection from *God Is Love*, Pope Benedict XVI offers a beautiful and inspiring look at the life resulting from a love of God and neighbor.

> **encyclical**
> a letter written by the Pope to the bishops about an area of Church teaching

Prayer is an important dimension of a loving relationship with God. Anthony Bloom's *Beginning to Pray* emphasizes prayer as an expression of a real relationship. Like all good relationships, prayer is a two-way street. Part of the problem with fashioning idols is that we mistakenly try to make God into a "thing." In the second reading, Bloom guides his readers around this pitfall in their prayer life. He maintains that prayer is a relationship with the living God, not with an instrument or tool—a thing—at our disposal that we can mechanically manipulate into serving our purposes. Before we begin to pray, Bloom asks us to consider serious questions: When God appears to be absent, would it be more honest to admit that we are absent from God? When we seek out the Lord, do we truly want God, or just something from God?

Excerpts from *God Is Love (Deus Caritas Est)*

by Pope Benedict XVI

Introduction

1. "God is love, and he who abides in love abides in God, and God abides in him" (*1 Jn* 4:16). These words from the *First Letter of John* express with remarkable clarity the heart of the Christian faith: the Christian image of God and the resulting image of mankind and its destiny. In the same verse, Saint John also offers a kind of

summary of the Christian life: "We have come to know and to believe in the love God has for us."

We have come to believe in God's love: in these words the Christian can express the fundamental decision of his life. Being Christian is not the result of an ethical choice or a lofty idea, but the encounter with an event, a person, which gives life a new horizon and a decisive direction. Saint John's Gospel describes that event in these words: "God so loved the world that he gave his only Son, that whoever believes in him should . . . have eternal life" (3:16). In acknowledging the centrality of love, Christian faith has retained the core of Israel's faith, while at the same time giving it new depth and breadth. The pious Jew prayed daily the words of the *Book of Deuteronomy* which expressed the heart of his existence: "Hear, O Israel: the Lord our God is one Lord, and you shall love the Lord your God with all your heart, and with all your soul and with all your might" (6:4–5). Jesus united into a single precept this commandment of love for God and the commandment of love for neighbour found in the *Book of Leviticus*: "You shall love your neighbour as yourself" (19:18; cf. *Mk* 12:29–31). Since God has first loved us (cf. *1 Jn* 4:10), love is now no longer a mere "command"; it is the response to the gift of love with which God draws near to us.

In a world where the name of God is sometimes associated with vengeance or even a duty of hatred and violence, this message is both timely and significant. For this reason, I wish in my first Encyclical to speak of the love which God lavishes upon us and which we in turn must share with others. . . .

Part I: The Unity of Love in Creation and in Salvation History

The newness of biblical faith

9. First, the world of the Bible presents us with a new image of God. In surrounding cultures, the image of God and of the gods ultimately remained unclear and contradictory. In the development of biblical faith, however, the content of the prayer fundamental to Israel, the *Shema*, became increasingly clear and unequivocal: "Hear, O Israel, the Lord our God is one Lord" (*Dt* 6:4). There is only one God, the Creator of

> **Shema**
>
> Hebrew word for "hear," used as the name of the prayer Jews recite daily at morning and evening services affirming the unity or oneness of God

heaven and earth, who is thus the God of all. Two facts are significant about this statement: all other gods are not God, and the universe in which we live has its source in God and was created by him. Certainly, the notion of creation is found elsewhere, yet only here does it become absolutely clear that it is not one god among many, but the one true God himself who is the source of all that exists; the whole world comes into existence by the power of his creative Word. Consequently, his creation is dear to him, for it was willed by him and "made" by him. The second important element now emerges: this God loves man. The divine power that Aristotle at the height of Greek philosophy sought to grasp through reflection, is indeed for every being an object of desire and of love— and as the object of love this divinity moves the world—

> **eros**
> a love based on desire

> **agape**
> unselfish, self-giving love; brotherly love

but in itself it lacks nothing and does not love: it is solely the object of love. The one God in whom Israel believes, on the other hand, loves with a personal love. His love, moreover, is an elective love: among all the nations he chooses Israel and loves her—but he does so precisely with a view to healing the whole human race. God loves, and his love may certainly be called *eros*, yet it is also totally *agape*.

The Prophets, particularly Hosea and Ezekiel, described God's passion for his people using boldly erotic images. God's relationship with Israel is described using the metaphors of betrothal and marriage; idolatry is thus adultery and prostitution. Here we find a specific reference . . . to the fertility cults and their abuse of *eros*, but also a description of the relationship of fidelity between Israel and her God. The history of the love-relationship between God and Israel consists, at the deepest level, in the fact that he gives her the *Torah*, thereby opening Israel's eyes to man's true nature and showing her the path leading to true humanism. It consists in the fact that man, through a life of fidelity to the one God, comes to experi-

> **Torah**
> general term for Jewish Law; also refers to the first five books of the Bible (the Pentateuch, the books of Moses), which contain the Law

ence himself as loved by God, and discovers joy in truth and in righteousness—a joy in God which becomes his essential happiness: "Whom do I have in heaven but you? And there is nothing upon earth that I desire besides you . . . for me it is good to be near God" (*Ps* 73 [72]:25, 28). . . .

Love of God and love of neighbour

16. Having reflected on the nature of love and its meaning in biblical faith, we are left with two questions concerning our own attitude: can we love God without seeing him? And can love be commanded? Against the double commandment of love these questions raise a double objection. No one has ever seen God, so how could we love him? Moreover, love cannot be commanded; it is ultimately a feeling that is either there or not, nor can it be produced by the will. Scripture seems to reinforce the first objection when it states: "If anyone says, 'I love God,' and hates his brother, he is a liar; for he who does not love his brother whom he has seen, cannot love God whom he has not seen" (*1 Jn* 4:20). But this text hardly excludes the love of God as something impossible. On the contrary, the whole context of the passage quoted from the *First Letter of John* shows that such love is explicitly demanded. The unbreakable bond between love of God and love of neighbour is emphasized. One is so closely connected to the other that to say that we love God becomes a lie if we are closed to our neighbour or hate him altogether. Saint John's words should rather be interpreted to mean that love of neighbour is a path that leads to the encounter

with God, and that closing our eyes to our neighbour also blinds us to God.

17. True, no one has ever seen God as he is. And yet God is not totally invisible to us; he does not remain completely inaccessible. God loved us first, says the *Letter of John* quoted above (cf. 4:10), and this love of God has appeared in our midst. He has become visible in as much as he "has sent his only Son into the world, so that we might live through him" (*1 Jn* 4:9). God has made himself visible: in Jesus we are able to see the Father (cf. *Jn* 14:9). Indeed, God is visible in a number of ways. In the love-story recounted by the Bible, he comes towards us, he seeks to win our hearts, all the way to the Last Supper, to the piercing of his heart on the Cross, to his appearances after the Resurrection and to the great deeds by which, through the activity of the Apostles, he guided the nascent Church along its path. Nor has the Lord been absent from subsequent Church history: he encounters us ever anew, in the men and women who reflect his presence, in his word, in the sacraments, and especially in the Eucharist. In the Church's Liturgy, in her prayer, in the living community of believers, we experience the love of God, we perceive his presence and we thus learn to recognize that presence in our daily lives. He has loved us first and he continues to do so; we too, then, can respond with love. God does not demand of us a feeling which we ourselves are incapable of producing. He loves us, he makes us see and experience his love, and since he has "loved us first," love can also blossom as a response within us. . . .

18. Love of neighbour is thus shown to be possible in the way proclaimed by the Bible, by Jesus. It consists

in the very fact that, in God and with God, I love even the person whom I do not like or even know. This can only take place on the basis of an intimate encounter with God, an encounter which has become a communion of will, even affecting my feelings. Then I learn to look on this other person not simply with my eyes and my feelings, but from the perspective of Jesus Christ. His friend is my friend. Going beyond exterior appearances, I perceive in others an interior desire for a sign of love, of concern. This I can offer them not only through the organizations intended for such purposes, accepting it perhaps as a political necessity. Seeing with the eyes of Christ, I can give to others much more than their outward necessities; I can give them the look of love which they crave. Here we see the necessary interplay between love of God and love of neighbour which the *First Letter of John* speaks of with such insistence. If I have no contact whatsoever with God in my life, then I cannot see in the other anything more than the other, and I am incapable of seeing in him the image of God. But if in my life I fail completely to heed others, solely out of a desire to be "devout" and to perform my "religious duties," then my relationship with God will also grow arid. It becomes merely "proper," but loveless. Only my readiness to encounter my neighbour and to show him love makes me sensitive to God as well. Only if I serve my neighbour can my eyes be opened to what God does for me and how much he loves me. The saints—consider the example of Blessed Teresa of Calcutta—constantly renewed their capacity for love of neighbour from their encounter with the Eucharistic Lord, and conversely this encounter acquired its realism and depth in their service to others. Love of God and love of neighbour are thus inseparable, they form a single commandment. But both live from the love of God who has loved us first. No longer is it a question, then, of a "commandment" imposed from without and calling for the impossible, but rather of a freely-bestowed experience of love from within, a love which by its very nature must then be shared with others. Love grows through love. Love is "divine" because it comes from God and unites us to God; through this unifying process it makes us a "we" which transcends our divisions and makes us one, until in the end God is "all in all" (*1 Cor* 15:28). . . .

Excerpt from *Beginning to Pray*

by Anthony Bloom

The Absence of God

. . . When we are aware of God, we stand before Him, worship Him, speak to Him.

At the outset there is, then, one very important problem: the situation of one for whom God seems to be absent. This is what I would like to speak about now. Obviously I am not speaking of a real absence—God is never really absent—but of the *sense* of absence which we have. We stand before God and we shout into an empty sky, out of which there is no reply. We turn in all directions and He is not to be found. What ought we to think of this situation?

First of all, it is very important to remember that prayer is an encounter and a relationship, a relationship which is deep, and this relationship cannot be forced either on us or on God. The fact that God can make Himself present or can leave us with the sense of His absence is part of this live and real relationship. If we could mechanically draw Him into an encounter, force Him to meet us, simply because we have chosen this moment to meet Him, there would be no relationship and no encounter. We can do that with an image, with the imagination, or with the various idols we can put in front of us instead of God; we can do nothing of the sort with the living God, any more than we can do it with a living person. A relationship must begin and develop in mutual freedom. If you look at the relationship in terms of *mutual* relationship, you will see that God could complain about us a great deal more than we about Him. We complain that He does not make Himself present to us for the few minutes we reserve for Him, but what about the twenty-three and a half hours during which God may be knocking at our door and we answer "I am busy, I am sorry" or when we do not answer at all because we do not even hear the knock at the door of our heart, of our minds, of our conscience, of our life. So there is a situation in which we have no right to complain of the absence of God, because we are a great deal more absent than He ever is.

The second very important thing is that a meeting face to face with God is always a moment of judgment for us. We cannot meet God in prayer or in meditation or in contemplation and not be either saved or condemned. I do not mean this in major terms of eternal damnation or eternal salvation already given and received, but it is always a critical moment, a crisis. "Crisis" comes from the Greek and means "judgment." To meet God face to face in prayer is a critical moment in our lives, and thanks be to Him that He does not always present Himself to us when we wish to meet Him, because we might not be able to endure such a meeting. Remember the many passages in Scripture in which we are told how bad it is to find oneself face to face with God, because God is power, God is truth, God is purity. Therefore, the first thought we ought to have when we do not tangibly perceive the divine presence, is a thought of gratitude. God is merciful; He does not come in an untimely way. He gives us a chance to judge ourselves, to understand, and not to come into His presence at a moment when it would mean condemnation.

I would like to give you an example of this. Many years ago a man came to see me. He asked me to show him God. I told him I could not but I added that even if I could, he would not be able to see Him, because I thought—and I do think—that to meet God one must have something in common with Him, something that gives you eyes to see, perceptiveness to perceive. He asked me then why I thought as I did, and I suggested that he should think a few moments and tell me whether there was any passage in the Gospel that moved him particularly, to see what was the connection between him and God. He said "Yes, in the eighth chapter of the Gospel according to St.

John, the passage concerning the woman taken in adultery." I said "Good, this is one of the most beautiful and moving passages. Now sit back and ask yourself, who are you in the scene which is described? Are you the Lord, or at least on His side, full of mercy, of understanding and full of faith in this woman who can repent and become a new creature? Are you the woman taken in adultery? Are you one of the older men who walk out at once because they are aware of their own sins, or one of the young ones who wait?" He thought for a few minutes then said "No, I feel I am the only Jew who would not have walked out but who would have stoned the woman." I said "Thank God that He does not allow you to meet Him face to face."

This may be an extreme example, but how often could we recognise similar situations in ourselves? Not that we flatly refuse God's word or God's example, but that in a less violent way we do what the soldiers did during the Passion. We would love to cover Christ's eyes, to be able to deal him blows freely without being seen. Do we not do this, to a certain extent, when we ignore the divine presence and act according to our own desires, our moods, contrary to everything which is God's will? We try to blind him, but in fact we blind ourselves. At such moments, how can we come into His presence? We can indeed, in repentance, broken-hearted; but we cannot come in the way in which we immediately wish to be received—with love, with friendship.

Look at the various passages in the Gospel. People much greater than ourselves hesitated to receive Christ. Remember the centurion who asked Christ to heal his servant. Christ said "I will come," but the centurion said "No, don't. Say a word and he will be healed." Do we do that? Do we turn to God and say "Don't make yourself tangibly, perceptively present before me. It is enough for You to say a word and I will be healed. It is enough for You to say a word and things *will* happen. I do not need more for the moment." Or take Peter in his boat after the great catch of fish, when he fell on his knees and said "Leave me, O Lord, I am a sinner." He asked the Lord to leave his boat because he felt humble—and he felt humble because he had suddenly perceived the greatness of Jesus. Do we ever do that? When we read the Gospel and the image of Christ becomes compelling, glorious, when we pray and we become aware of the greatness, the holiness of God, do we ever say "I am unworthy that He should come near me"? Not to speak of all the occasions when we should be aware that He cannot come to us because we are not there to receive Him. We want something *from* Him, not *Him* at all. Is that a relationship? Do we behave in that way with our friends? Do we aim at what friendship can *give* us or is it the friend whom we love? Is this true with regard to the Lord?

Let us think of our prayers, yours and mine; think of the warmth, the depth and intensity of your prayer when it concerns someone you love or something which matters to your life. Then your heart is open, all your inner self is recollected in the prayer. Does it mean that God matters to you? No, it does not. It simply means that the subject matter of your prayer matters to you. For when you have made your passionate, deep, intense prayer concerning the person you love or the situation that worries you, and you turn to the next item, which does not matter so much—if you suddenly grow cold, what has changed? Has God grown cold? Has He gone? No, it means that all the elation, all the intensity in your prayer was not born of God's presence, of your faith in Him, of your longing for Him, of your awareness of Him; it was born of nothing but your concern for him or her or it, not for God. How can we feel surprised, then, that this absence of God affects us? It is we who make ourselves absent, it is we who grow cold the moment we are no longer concerned with God. Why? Because He does not matter so much.

There are other ways too in which God is "absent." As long as we ourselves are real, as long as we are truly ourselves, God can be present and can do something with us. But the moment we try to be what we are not, there is nothing left to say or have; we become a fictitious personality, an unreal presence, and this unreal presence cannot be approached by God.

In order to be able to pray, we must be within the situation which is defined as the kingdom of God. We must recognise that He is God, that He is King, we must surrender to Him. We must at least be concerned with His will, even if we are not yet capable of fulfilling it. But if we are not, if we treat God like the rich young man who could not follow Christ because he was too rich, then how can we meet Him? So often what we would like to have through prayer, through

> ### Kingdom of God
> the subject of most of Jesus's parables, usually likened to surprising activity that surpasses expectations; the world as God wants it to be; the ideal state of affairs

the deep relationship with God which we long for, is simply another period of happiness; we are not prepared to sell all that we have in order to buy the pearl of great price. Then how should we get this pearl of great price? Is that what we expect to get? Is it not the same as in human relationships: when a man or a woman experiences love for another, other people no longer matter in the same way. To put it in a short formula from the ancient world, "When a man has a bride, he is no longer surrounded by men and women, but by people."

Isn't that what could, what should happen with regard to all our riches when we turn to God? Surely they should become pale and grey, just a general background against which the only figure that matters would appear in intense relief? We would like just one touch of heavenly blue in the general picture of our life, in which there are so many dark sides. God is prepared to be outside it, He is prepared to take it up completely as a cross, but He is not prepared to be simply part of our life.

For Reflection

1. What are some of the false gods in our society that compete for our attention and devotion? Identify three and explain the "false promises" they make.

2. What does it mean to have someone choose to love you as opposed to being obligated to love you? How does our relationship with God change when we choose to return the love God gives us?

3. What does Anthony Bloom mean when he writes, "We cannot meet God in prayer or in meditation or in contemplation and not be either saved or condemned"? Write a paragraph explaining your answer.

4. Like the man who came to visit Bloom, select a Gospel passage that is particularly moving to you. Write a brief essay describing why you selected this passage, who you are in the scene that you selected, and how that might describe your relationship with God.

Endnotes

1. *Mt* 22:37; cf. *Lk* 10:27: ". . . and with all your strength."
2. *Deut* 6:4.

4

The Second Commandment: "You shall not make wrongful use of the name of the LORD your God."

Among all the words of Revelation, there is one which is unique: the revealed name of God. God confides his name to those who believe in him; he reveals himself to them in his personal mystery. The gift of a name belongs to the order of trust and intimacy. "The Lord's name is holy." For this reason man must not abuse it. He must keep it in mind in silent, loving adoration. He will not introduce it into his own speech except to bless, praise, and glorify it.[1] (*CCC*, no. 2143)

Introduction

The second commandment's prohibition against taking the Lord's name in vain may strike you as puzzling or even trivial. If so, this is probably due to the perception that it simply forbids cursing, vulgarities, and other violations of etiquette. For the ancient Israelites, this commandment—important enough to be one of only ten—pertained to a matter far more serious than good manners. The Lord's name goes to the heart of God's relationship with God's people. For that reason the name is to be cherished, not abused.

There is power in language (in Genesis, chapter 1, God creates by speaking) and special significance in a name and the privilege of naming. When God created the animals, he brought each one to Adam to be named (Genesis 2:19–20). Today, parents name their children. It reflects a hierarchy in the order of creation and implies the responsibility to care for those one names. Conversely, it is customary to show respect by referring to elders or superiors by their title and last name, rather than assuming the familiarity of using their first name. Consider the story of the burning bush and how Moses's request for God's name would be understood (Exodus, chapter 3). In the encounter at the burning bush, God entrusts God's name to Moses. It is an unexpected invitation to intimacy, a show of trust that is not to be betrayed.

In *The Law of Christ*, Bernard Häring, CSSR, presents moral theology's traditional approach to reverencing the name of God. He explores the various ways people can honor or abuse the divine name in speech, but his entire treatment is based on the sacred nature of the relationship between God and God's people. Profanity, blasphemy, and false oaths are problematic because they disrespect the most intimate and personal of relationships.

Furthermore, by directing respect for the Lord's name, the second commandment attempts to safeguard our understanding of God. The commandment recognizes the fact that a full understanding of God is beyond our comprehension. We can never completely describe God or encapsulate his glory in the words we use. Thus, speaking of God requires humility if it is not to be "vain" talk or empty chatter.

Matt McDonald explores the contemporary relevance of this humility. He finds that all too often we begin to identify God with our purposes and opinions. Along these lines we are easily mistaken. After all, God said, "I Am Who I Am," not "I Am Who you want me to be." McDonald sums this up with the observation that God is "bigger" than we are. He concludes by suggesting that we focus on our journey with God, rather than trying to define God prematurely, and remember who is the creator and who is the created in our relationship with God.

Excerpts from *The Law of Christ: Moral Theology for Priests and Laity*

by Bernard Häring, CSSR

II. REVERENCE FOR THE HOLY NAME OF GOD
    1. *Religious Significance of the Divine Name*
    a. . . . The revelation of the divine name, *Yahweh,* is a most solemn moment in the history of salvation (Ex 3:13ff.). Through the name, "The God of our fathers . . . ," God reveals Himself to Moses in His uniqueness and unequivocally as the God of sacred history and the Lord of the ages. With the supreme name of Yahweh, God reveals that He Himself is the "Mighty-Helper." The pro-

phetic names of the Messiah
("Emmanuel," Is 7:14; cf. Mt
1:23; "Wonder-Counsellor,"
"God-Hero," "Father-Forever,"
"Prince of Peace" in Is 9:5;
"Jesus" in Mt 1:21) focus

> **Yahweh**
> proper name for God in the
> Jewish scriptures, from the
> Hebrew verb "to be"

attention on the most characteristic qualities and activities
of Christ, the "Anointed One." To invoke the name of the
Lord is to call upon Him as present.

b. The name is the basis of a new relationship, of
dependence and protection. According to Genesis 2:19f.,
Adam gave the names to all the animals as they appeared
before him. This means, in the first place, that he correctly discerned the nature of things and, secondly, that
he fulfilled the divine mandate to "have dominion over"
all the beasts of the earth. Designating lands or cities by
new names is often attestation of their subjection through
conquest or submissive acceptance of protection (cf. 2 Sm
12:28). In times of public disaster every woman would
desperately seek a husband, begging to become his by
receiving his name (Is 4:1).

Yahweh calls Israel by name and on this act bases his
title to her love and fidelity to Him (Is 43:1). The name
of Yahweh is invoked over Israel to express the divine
dominion and protection (Is 63:19; 2 Par 7:14). The holy
name of Yahweh is invoked over the temple (Jer 7:10ff.),
over the ark of the covenant (2 Sm 6:2), and over Jerusa-
lem (Jer 25:29; Dn 9:18f.). Thereby they become "holy,"
consecrated to the Lord; they belong to Him. The invoca-
tion of the divine name is the source of the confidence in
the special protection of God (cf. Jer 14:9: "thy holy name

is invoked over us;" *nomen sanctum tuum invocatum est super nos,* the Church prays in her evensong). "Whoever calls upon the name of the Lord," that is to say, whoever places himself under the dominion and protection of God, "shall be saved" (Acts 2:21; cf. Rom 10:13). . . .

c. In revealing His name God manifests His love for us and His desire to enter into communion with us.

All the divine names in the Old Testament point to the providential offer of God's tender care and love for man. But this revelation of the divine name reaches its climax in the manifestation of the name of God as Father brought to us through Christ: "Father . . . I have manifested thy name to the men whom thou hast given me out of the world" (Jn 17:1–6). The fact that God Himself has revealed His name to us and invited us to invoke it gives to our prayer an assurance which is absolutely unique.

> **providential**
>
> pertaining to God's all-knowing and loving ordering of events

To know one by name and call him by name is a sign of trust and familiarity. Jesus the Good Shepherd knows and calls His sheep "by name" (Jn 10:3). Similarly it is a sign of our intimacy with God through grace that we are so much as allowed to call Him "by name." And since the name is that of Father, there is enclosed in the name the incomparable gift of intimate trust by which we are admitted to the inner community of divine love which is the Trinity itself.

d. The name (*shem*) in the Old Testament often designates the person of God. The name of God stands for God Himself. His name is assurance of His presence and His help. "Behold I will send my angel, who shall go before thee . . . my name is in him" (Ex 23:20f.).

e. The name of God stands for the honor and glory of God. "My name (i.e. my honor) is great among the nations" (Mal 1:11). The words in the Our Father are similar: "Hallowed be thy name." Here *name* is practically equivalent to *honor,* but it connotes something further, above all the loving will of God. The words in Malachias, "Everywhere they bring sacrifice in my name, and a pure offering" clearly reveal the bond between the name of God and the divine worship. This corresponds to the intimate relationship between the two concepts, honor and glory of God and the divine cult or worship of God. . . .

The name of God, which is associated essentially with the love of God for men and the revealed will of God inviting men to a community of fellowship with Him, also connotes something of the honor and glory (*dóxa*) of God. This is particularly apparent in the Gospel according to John. "Father, glorify thy name!" "I have both glorified it, and I will glorify (*doxázein*) it again" (Jn 12:28). The heavenly Father glorifies His name most of all through the

> **Passion**
> Jesus's suffering after the Last Supper leading up to his death

manifestation of His Fatherly love in Christ, particularly in the passion and resurrection. Tenderly and lovingly He reveals His glory and honor by showing and proving that He is truly our Father. Hence, the proper use of the name of God implies homage to the majesty of God. If that which is ultimate in the revelation of the divine name is the manifestation of God as our Father, it must follow that every divine name can be properly spoken and truly honored only through the expression and inner spirit befitting the name of one's Father. In every name of God we must honor Him as our Father: this means, pronunciation with loving reverence. We pronounce every divine name, including the names which reveal the loving majesty and glory of God (particularly the words, *Cross* and *Holy Sacrament*) with this veneration and love. . . .

3. *Misuse of the Holy Name*

Apart from inculpable imperfection in the degree of love and reverence owing to God in His holy name, there are various stages or degrees of dishonor shown to the sacred name of God, ranging from profane language (using the name "in vain") to diabolic disdain or scorn for it.

> **inculpable**
> without blame or guilt

> **profane**
> mundane and ordinary; not set aside for holy purposes; irreverent or contemptuous of God

It is contrary to the reverence and love due to the name of God to refer to Him and the loving majesty of His holy name in the same vein as one speaks of profane sciences. It is not reverential to refer to God lightly as "he" or "it."

Sometimes we note the use of such terms as "the deity," as though God were some far-off thing. If we must not only speak to God in prayer but also about Him, for the simple reason that the very enunciation of His holy name is a special tribute of honor paid to it, then surely our speech must be filled with loving reverence. There must always be something of sacred jubilation, of tender and reverent intimacy, of loving friendship implied in the direct address which refers to God as "Thou." . . .

The sin of "vain use" of holy names, often called profane language, is in all its forms a venial sin (*ex genere suo veniale*). But the forbearance of theologians for human frailty, evident in the mildness of their censure of this species of abuse of the holy names, does not warrant the conclusion that it is not important to fight against the evil of profane language or to overcome the habit if one has fallen into it. A truly interior reverence for God, perfect worship of God in spirit and in truth, is utterly incompatible with any misuse of the holy names.

> **venial sin**
> a less serious sin (compared to a mortal sin)

> **censure**
> official disapproval or condemnation

It is essentially more malicious to misuse the name of God as an expression or manifestation of emotions which are in themselves disordered and sinful, as for example feelings of vexation and impatience, unrestrained or unjust anger. Nevertheless, we must make a distinction: the sacred names may be uttered merely on the occasion of sinful emotion or violent outburst of feeling. They may be blurted out without thought or reflection or by force of habit. But, on the other hand, they may be consciously

> **malicious**
> deliberately harmful

> **vexation**
> irritation or annoyance

and intentionally employed for the very purpose of venting base emotions or even to give vile passions a kind of hypocritical respectability or sacredness.

"In Our Image"

by Matt McDonald

Growing up, when my brothers and I found ourselves in one of our minutiae-obsessed, pop-trivia-fueled discussions and a question came up about a fact pertaining to whatever it was we were discussing, one of us always seemed to know the answer

minutiae

minor or trivial details

right away. You may want to read that last sentence again and notice the word *seemed*. A better word might be *acted*. One of us would consistently turn up a for-certain answer to even the most bizarre questions, and they usually sounded like we were just making them up. If I was suspicious that one of my brothers was doing this, I would press him for details about where he got his information. His response usually went something like, "It just is."

"But how do you know?" I would say.

"I just do. It's just common knowledge."

And when I was lucky, I would dig at him until I discovered the truth—that he was making an assumption that sounded very much like it could probably be true, but that may or may not actually be true. In other words, it sounded right. It made sense that it could be right, but it was only something that he had decided on for himself with little foundation in actual fact.

Spending as much time in church as I do, I see a lot of people who are very certain about God. Not just that He exists, or that His Biblical truths are, in fact, true—most everybody agrees on those things. What I'm talking about is a certainty about who God *really* is; a surefire interpretation of the person, personality, sense of humor and political affiliation of the almighty, omniscient Being who thought us up in the first place. How the sculpture could ever understand the artist is beyond me, but somehow we seem to have gotten it all figured out.

narcissist
one who feels excessive self-love

It has always fascinated me how everybody has a different interpretation of God. To some, He is an old, white-haired, deep-south Republican. To some, God is a hippie (what with His whole "love everybody equally" thing). To some, He is little more than Santa Claus. To others still, He is a narcissist, a madman. And all of these people are 100 percent sure that their convictions and interpretations are right, and that God is who they say He is.

And let's not stop with the most extreme examples. Let's remember that some people also like to claim to know exactly what style of music God prefers, and exactly how He'd like us to dress. They know exactly who is and who is not in God's favor judging by the simple criteria of whether or not these people listen to Christian music and read the right translation of the Bible.

And in all of this, I have trouble with one seemingly simple concept: understanding exactly who God is. Sometimes I get the feeling that God is like that old friend that I haven't seen for a while, and who I remember as acting, talking and thinking a certain way. But when I run into my old friend and talk to him again, I realize that the way I remember him is only a stylized version of his real self. I realize that his true personality is much more layered and complex than my memory of him, and that I don't really know him that well after all.

To come to a clearer understanding of the person of God, we have to consider that perhaps we have made God out in our minds to be something that He is not. We have filled in the gaps in our understanding of Him and compensated for our lack of a physical God model by constructing Him in our minds as someone who looks, acts, thinks and believes just like we want Him to—just like us. If people in our past have manipulated His word to justify murder, racism, misogyny and innumerable other sins, how much more easily can we manipulate it to fit our political, theological, philosophical and personal beliefs?

Our problem with understanding God has to do with our size when compared to His. He is enormous. He made us. All of our words and thoughts and methods of understanding things—even Him—come from Him. We can do nothing apart from His presence. So then it stands to reason that because of this, our understanding of Him will always be incomplete. We can understand the concepts of this world, the tiniest details of science and math that we live among, because we are separate from them. Between us and those things there is a distance that gives us power over them. We can grab an atom out of thin air and split it. We can set up workstations in space. We can transplant live organs from one human to another. But we can never understand God in the same way that the things we create can never understand us.

The sadness in this situation is that rather than accepting His superiority over us, we have to use what we know from our own experience to understand Him. And that experience will always be incomplete and biased. The truth, as they say, is out there. God is who He is regardless of what we think of Him. If only we could let go of what we want to believe and get our heads around the fact that we will never figure Him out completely, and that the journey is as important as the destination.

For Reflection

1. How does the name Yahweh help us better understand God? What are other titles we use for God? List three other titles for God and explain the image of God they provide.

2. How is the proper use of someone's name a sign of respect? What are examples in our society in which we use titles and proper names to show respect?

3. How does the misuse of God's name display a lack of understanding of who God is and our relationship with God? Explain.

4. How does the second commandment relate to the use of God's name for personal gain or to pass judgment on others? Identify a situation in our society where you see the misuse of God's name for personal gain. Explain.

Endnotes

1. Cf. *Zech* 2:13; Ps 29:2, 113:1–2.

5

The Third Commandment: "Remember the sabbath day, and keep it holy."

On Sundays and other holy days of obligation, the faithful are to refrain from engaging in work or activities that hinder the worship owed to God, the joy proper to the Lord's Day, the performance of the works of mercy, and the appropriate relaxation of mind and body.[1] (*CCC*, no. 2185)

Introduction

Released July 5, 1998, John Paul II's apostolic letter *On Keeping Sunday Holy (Dies Domini:* literally, "Day of the Lord"; also known as "On Keeping the Lord's Day Holy") addresses a contemporary crisis within the Church. In many parts of the world, Mass attendance is in decline. This means not only that people are failing to take advantage of the opportunity to develop their relationship with God that the Holy Eucharist presents, but also that they may lose the connection the Eucharist has to the rest of their lives throughout the week. Amidst the distractions of modern life, John Paul II's letter invites the people of the Church to keep Sunday holy.

On Keeping Sunday Holy clearly distinguishes Sunday worship from both the historical Sabbath and the weekend. The Sabbath that the third commandment instructs the Israelites to "keep holy" is Saturday, the seventh and final day of the week. God established it in the order of things by resting on that day after completing the work of Creation. It creates a sacred space and time for rest when the week's work is done. Christian observance moved to Sunday, the first day of the week, because it is the day of Jesus's Resurrection. Christians look upon Sunday as the fulfillment of the Sabbath. Sunday worship ushers in a new week, just as Jesus's redeeming work brings about a "new creation."

John Paul II insists that the Sabbath day of rest is not to be confused with the weekend. While the weekend is for relaxation, the Sabbath has a much more profound meaning of freeing people from oppressive work. It is an observation tied to the commemoration of the Passover and liberation from slavery (Deuteronomy 5:15). Therefore the Pope directs our attention to the many who, because of low wages, unfair work conditions, and systemic injustice, are not free to rest and asks us to stand in solidarity with them.

Moreover, the Mass and even Sunday as a whole is a time for deepening our relationship with the Lord. Indeed, John Paul II reminds us not only of our obligation to attend weekly Mass but also that going to church each week is not sufficient to "keep holy the Sabbath." Sunday should fill our week, our entire life with meaning. This entails spending time in prayer, with family, and in the work of charity. In fact, John Paul II is careful to emphasize this last point. Sunday cannot be confused with weekend relaxation because it exists as both a day for rest and a day for the works of mercy.

In "Let's Put the Eucharist to Work," Robert McClory is concerned with the observation that those who attend Mass on Sunday, far too frequently do not act anything like Christians throughout the rest of the week. His essay explores the ways in which the Eucharist is nourishing true Christian living in various communities.

Pope John Paul II and Robert McClory agree that the third commandment requires much more than church attendance. As a result, they issue an invitation to deeper, richer participation in the life of the church community. A spiritual life characterized not just by piety, but also by the struggle for justice, is one that both authors argue is much more in keeping with the meaning of the Eucharist.

Excerpts from *On Keeping Sunday Holy (Dies Domini)*

by Pope John Paul II

4. Until quite recently, it was easier in traditionally Christian countries to keep Sunday holy because it was an almost universal practice and because, even in the organization of civil society, Sunday rest was considered a fixed part of the work schedule. Today, however, even in those countries which give legal sanction to the festive character of Sunday, changes in socioeconomic conditions have

often led to profound modifications of social behaviour and hence of the character of Sunday. The custom of the "weekend" has become more widespread, a weekly period of respite, spent perhaps far from home and often involving participation in cultural, political or sporting activities which are usually held on free days. This social and cultural phenomenon is by no means without its positive aspects if, while respecting true values, it can contribute to people's development and to the advancement of the life of society as a whole. All of this responds not only to the need for rest, but also to the need for celebration which is inherent in our humanity. Unfortunately, when Sunday loses its fundamental meaning and becomes merely part of a "weekend," it can happen that people stay locked within a horizon so limited that they can no longer see "the heavens." Hence, though ready to celebrate, they are really incapable of doing so.

> **sanction**
> official approval

The disciples of Christ, however, are asked to avoid any confusion between the celebration of Sunday, which should truly be a way of keeping the Lord's Day holy, and the "weekend," understood as a time of simple rest and relaxation. This will require a genuine spiritual maturity, which will enable Christians to "be what they are," in full accordance with the gift of faith, always ready to give an account of the hope which is in them (cf. 1 *Pt* 3:15). In this way, they will be led to a deeper understanding of Sunday, with the result that,

> **docility**
> trait of being easily taught or trained

even in difficult situations, they will be able to live it in complete docility to the Holy Spirit. . . .

The Fulfilment of the Sabbath . . .

61. As the seventh day blessed and consecrated by God, the "shabbat" concludes the whole work of creation, and is therefore immediately linked to the work of the sixth day when God made man "in his image and likeness" (cf. *Gn* 1:26). This very close connection between the "day of God" and the "day of man" did not escape the Fathers in their meditation on the biblical creation story. Saint Ambrose says in this regard: "Thanks, then, to the Lord our God who accomplished a work in which he might find rest. He made the heavens, but I do not read that he found rest there; he made the stars, the moon, the sun, and neither do I read that he found rest in them. I read instead that he made man and that then he rested, finding in man one to whom he could offer the forgiveness of sins." Thus there will be for ever a direct link between the "day of God" and the "day of man." When the divine commandment declares: "Remember the Sabbath day in order to keep it holy" (*Ex* 20:8), the rest decreed in order to honour the day dedicated to God is not at all a burden imposed upon man, but

> **consecrated**
> made sacred and dedicated to a purpose

> **shabbat**
> Hebrew word for the Jewish Sabbath

rather an aid to help him to recognize his life-giving and liberating dependence upon the Creator, and at the same time his calling to cooperate in the Creator's work and to receive his grace. In honouring God's "rest," man fully discovers himself, and thus the Lord's Day bears the profound imprint of God's blessing (cf. *Gn* 2:3), by virtue of which, we might say, it is endowed in a way similar to the animals and to man himself, with a kind of "fruitfulness" (cf. *Gn* 1:22, 28). This "fruitfulness" is apparent above all in filling and, in a certain sense, "multiplying" time itself, deepening in men and women the joy of living and the desire to foster and communicate life. . . .

63. Christ came to accomplish a new "exodus," to restore freedom to the oppressed. He performed many healings on the Sabbath (cf. *Mt* 12:9–14 and parallels), certainly not to violate the Lord's Day, but to reveal its full meaning: "The Sabbath was made for man, not man for the Sabbath" (*Mk* 2:27). Opposing the excessively legalistic interpretation of some of his contemporaries, and developing the true meaning of the biblical Sabbath, Jesus, as "Lord of the Sabbath" (*Mk* 2:28), restores to the Sabbath observance its liberating character, carefully safeguarding the rights of God and the rights of man. This is why Christians, called as they are to proclaim the liberation won by the blood of Christ, felt that they had the authority to transfer the meaning of the Sabbath to the day of the Resurrection. The Passover of Christ has in fact liberated man from a slavery more radi-

> **legalistic**
> rigidly adhering to rules

cal than any weighing upon an oppressed people—the slavery of sin, which alienates man from God, and alienates man from himself and from others, constantly sowing within history the seeds of evil and violence.

The day of rest

64. For several centuries, Christians observed Sunday simply as a day of worship, without being able to give it the specific meaning of Sabbath rest. Only in the fourth century did the civil law of the Roman Empire recognize the weekly recurrence, determining that on "the day of the sun" the judges, the people of the cities and the various trade corporations would not work. Christians rejoiced to see thus removed the obstacles which until then had sometimes made observance of the Lord's Day heroic. They could now devote themselves to prayer in common without hindrance.

It would therefore be wrong to see in this legislation of the rhythm of the week a mere historical circumstance with no special significance for the Church and which she could simply set aside. Even after the fall of the Empire, the Councils did not cease to insist upon the arrangements regarding Sunday rest. In countries where Christians are in the minority and where the festive days of the calendar do not coincide with Sunday, it is still Sunday which remains the Lord's Day, the day on which the faithful come together for the Eucharistic assembly. But this involves real sacrifices. For Christians it is not normal that Sunday, the day of joyful celebration, should not also be a day of rest, and it is difficult for them to keep Sunday holy if they do not have enough free time. . . .

A day of solidarity

69. Sunday should also give the faithful an opportunity to devote themselves to works of mercy, charity and apostolate. To experience the joy of the Risen Lord deep within is to share fully the love which pulses in his heart: there is no joy without love! Jesus himself explains this, linking the "new commandment" with the gift of joy: "If you keep my commandments, you will remain in my love, just as I have kept the Father's commandments and remain in his love. I have told you this that my own joy may be in you and your joy may be complete. This is my commandment: that you love one another as I have loved you" (*Jn* 15:10–12).

> **solidarity**
> unity of feeling, interest, and purpose among people that promotes justice

> **apostolate**
> the work of promoting religious teaching

The Sunday Eucharist, therefore, not only does not absolve the faithful from the duties of charity, but on the contrary commits them even more "to all the works of charity, of mercy, of apostolic outreach, by means of which it is seen that the faithful of Christ are not of this world and yet are the light of the world, giving glory to the Father in the presence of men." . . .

> **apostolic**
> characteristic of an apostle

72. The Eucharist is an event and programme of true brotherhood. From the Sunday Mass there flows a tide of charity destined to spread into the whole life of the faithful, beginning by inspiring the very way in which they live the rest of Sunday. If Sunday is a day of joy, Christians should declare by their actual behaviour that we cannot be happy "on our own." They look around to find people who may need their help. It may be that in their neighbourhood or among those they know there are sick people, elderly people, children or immigrants who precisely on Sundays feel more keenly their isolation, needs and suffering. It is true that commitment to these people cannot be restricted to occasional Sunday gestures. But presuming a wider sense of commitment, why not make the Lord's Day a more intense time of sharing, encouraging all the inventiveness of which Christian charity is capable? Inviting to a meal people who are alone, visiting the sick, providing food for needy families, spending a few hours in voluntary work and acts of solidarity: these would certainly be ways of bringing into people's lives the love of Christ received at the Eucharistic table.

73. Lived in this way, not only the Sunday Eucharist but the whole of Sunday becomes a great school of charity, justice and peace. The presence of the Risen Lord in the midst of his people becomes an undertaking of solidarity, a compelling force for inner renewal, an inspiration to change the structures of sin in which individuals, communities and at times entire peoples are entangled. Far from being an escape, the Christian Sunday is a "prophecy" inscribed on time itself, a prophecy obliging the faithful to follow in the footsteps of the One who came

"to preach good news to the poor, to proclaim release to captives and new sight to the blind, to set at liberty those who are oppressed, and to proclaim the acceptable year of the Lord" (*Lk* 4:18–19). In the Sunday commemoration of Easter, believers learn from Christ, and remembering his promise: "I leave you peace, my peace I give you" (*Jn* 14:27), they become in their turn *builders of peace.*

Excerpts from "Let's Put the Eucharist to Work"

by Robert J. McClory

Is the Eucharist working? It may seem a strange question, but it's one that is worth asking, especially this year, the Year of the Eucharist in the Catholic Church.

Some have been claiming for a long time that the Eucharist is not working because of published reports that most Catholics no longer believe the bread and wine really become the Body and Blood, soul and divinity of Jesus Christ.

Critics point to the absence of "eucharistic piety" they observe among Mass-goers: failure to genuflect when entering or leaving the church, the routine way people come up to receive Communion, the casual conversations right in front of the tabernacle after Mass. And so the church

> **Benediction**
> a short service involving the blessing of the congregation with the Eucharistic host

has undertaken a worldwide effort this year to educate Catholics about the nature of the Eucharist and to promote devotions such as visits to the Blessed Sacrament, Benediction, perpetual adoration, even public eucharistic processions and rallies.

Others see the issue differently. That some Catholics fail to believe Christ is truly present in the form of bread and wine is lamentable, they agree. But even more lamentable, they insist, is that great numbers of Catholics, including many whose devotion to the Eucharist is rock solid, fail to grasp the intimate connection between the Eucharist and justice, between Christ present in the bread and wine and what we do or don't do in the world around us.

Dangerous Disconnect

Almost 25 years ago the late liturgist Father Robert Hovda put it this way: "Our habits and our predetermined ways and the structures of our society have fastened such blinders on our harnesses that, as a whole, Christians and Christian churches in our society have only the haziest notion of any moral imperative flowing from the Sunday meeting in which we celebrate God's word of human liberation and solidarity and then act it out in the breaking of the bread and the sharing of the cup. As obvious as those ethical demands are, they simply do not impinge, they do not get through to us. We are too well protected by the world we live in."

Hovda said the Eucharist isn't working as it should because it has been "domesticated." He cited the anguished words of a Sri Lankan bishop, who wrote: "Why is it that in spite of hundreds of thousands of eucharistic celebrations Christians continue as selfish as before? Why is the gap of income, wealth, knowledge, and power growing in the world today—and that in favor of the Christian peoples? Why is it that persons who proclaim eucharistic love and sharing deprive the poor of the world of food, capital, employment, even land?"

The Eucharist, whether seen as Holy Communion or as the Mass, can become "a kind of product created for individual spiritual customers," says Gabe Huck, a veteran liturgist and former director of Liturgy Training Publications. "It's supposed to have a transforming effect on us," he says, "so that we leave church determined to do something. We should be seeing the world in a different way and have different priorities because of the Eucharist. It should affect what we do with our time, how we spend our money, how we look for a job, how we vote."

This message of a transformative connection between Eucharist and responsibility to the world may be communicated at many parishes in only the vaguest way. In others, however, where a concerted effort is made, the message is getting through. . . .

Money Where Their Mouth Is

In Arvada, Colorado, a suburb of Denver, Spirit of Christ Catholic Community makes the connection in several dramatic ways. First, parishioners are informed that it is a "stewardship community," which means 14 percent off the top of the Sunday collections goes to the poor and needy. And at this parish of about 3,300 mostly upper-middle-class families, 14 percent amounts to about $300,000 a year.

Kathi Palitano, director of pastoral ministry, says recent recipients include groups digging wells in Nicaragua, providing care for AIDS orphans in Africa, and serving the homeless in the Arvada area. "It's a demanding process for us and the applicants," she says, "but it ensures the funds are going to responsible people."

> **stewardship**
> making good use of the things entrusted to one's care

Second, the parish has a "Southern Exposure" program, which so far has involved 40 groups of parishioners in constructing from scratch 150 homes in poverty-stricken areas of Mexico.

Third, some 800 parishioners participate in 80 small faith groups that discuss how the Sunday lectionary readings relate to their life in the world. Then there are the 400 persons involved in liturgical and other ministries, says Janette Fayhoe, liturgy director. And the parish's adult education forum brings in high-caliber guest speakers like Sister Helen Prejean and Bishop Thomas Gumbleton.

This intense activity is successful, says the pastor, Father Robert Kinkel, because "everything we do is presented as flowing directly from the Eucharist; the connection is in the homilies, the intercessions, the music."

What helps make it all come together, he adds, is the location of the altar—right in the midst of the assembly. "Everyone can see what we have here," he says, "the Body of Christ celebrating the Body of Christ."

Beyond Jesus-and-Me

At Our Lady of the Most Holy Rosary in Albuquerque, New Mexico, the pieces are also in place. The pews are in a horseshoe shape around the altar "so the visibility is wonderful and there's no last row where people can hide," says the Norbertine pastor, Father Joel Garner. In addition, this parish of 2,500 families has "the best and most active" St. Vincent DePaul Society in the region, a commitment to small faith communities, and a determination to link the Eucharist to the larger world.

The parishioners, about 85 percent of whom are later-generation Americans of Mexican descent, are attracted to an older, more devotional Catholicism. The church has overnight adoration of the Blessed Sacrament once a month. "That sometimes is where their energy goes—that and the veneration of the saints. This is what the people were taught to do," says Garner. The result, he says, can be a Jesus-and-me spirituality that he does not want to stifle, yet he and the staff hope to open it to wider horizons.

One strategy the staff has developed is a vigorous welcoming approach designed to push people beyond personal concerns and into the wider community. The most visible sign of this is the requirement that before Mass eucharistic ministers stand at the doors and welcome churchgoers with smiles and handshakes. "A lot of newcomers are not used to such greetings," says Christina Spahn, pastoral associate for faith formation, "but they come to appreciate it."

Consciousness-raising is also evident in the Pax Christi group now in formation; in the Mass intercessions, which relate to needs in and well beyond the parish; and in the parish's 12-year relationship with Albuquerque Interfaith, which promotes grassroots conversations and cooperative action in the city.

True Authenticity

Parishes like these are attempting to put into practice what Vatican II's Constitution on the Sacred Liturgy called for: "full, conscious, and active participation in the liturgy," since it is "the indispensable source of the Christian spirit." A booklet on the Year of the Eucharist published by the U.S. Conference of Catholic Bishops highlights the social dimensions of the Eucharist, citing the late Pope John Paul II's declaration that the Eucharist fosters "a social love in which we put the common good ahead of private food, take up the cause of the community, the parish, the universal church, and extend our charity to the whole world."

In his apostolic letter inaugurating the eucharistic year, John Paul was even more pointed: "We mustn't deceive ourselves; it's from our reciprocal love and, in particular, from the concern we have for those in need that we will be recognized as true disciples of Christ. This is the criterion on the basis of which the authenticity of the eucharistic celebrations will be confirmed."

As several commentators quickly noted, use of the word "authenticity" with regard to the Eucharist almost always refers to carrying out the proper liturgical regulations. Yet here is John Paul asserting that, even if all the liturgical protocols have been satisfied, the Eucharist is not "authentic" unless it is related to those in need. . . .

You Are What You Eat

The predominantly African American parishioners are also the link in two churches in inner-city New Orleans. At both Our Lady Star of the Sea and St. Philip the Apostle, the communities are bedeviled by gang activity, unemployment, and joblessness.

"So when they hear that the Son of Man had nowhere to lay his head," says Father R. Tony Ricard, pastor of both parishes, "they know what that means. A lot of them have been evicted from their homes a time or two themselves. They know suffering just as Jesus did."

Ricard says his churches sponsor exposition of the Blessed Sacrament only one day a year, Holy Thursday, because he wants people to realize they are the tabernacles of the Eucharist. That's what he preaches in and out of season: "If you are what you eat, and if you receive the Eucharist over and over for years, then just about every cell in your body has been nourished with it. That's who you are! You bring Jesus' body and blood out into the world."

Ricard is also striving to bring the world, especially young people, to the Eucharist. Besides the usual variety of sports and other youth activities, Ricard draws substantial numbers of teens directly into liturgical participation.

"On Youth Sunday," he says, "we might have 70 or 80 up around the altar—there's the youth choir and the junior ushers and the ministers of hospitality and the readers and the dancers (we call them the movement team), and maybe eight or more servers." When the young participate, he believes, they're inclined to take more seriously what the church is all about, and so are their parents and other relatives.

Following up on this activity, Ricard and his staff recruit parishioners young and old for community ministries, including neighborhood cleanup and efforts to demand accountability from local elected leaders and city officials. Participation in liturgy and creating a better world are part of the same thing, he says, "and our people know it."

Making a Difference

So is the Eucharist working? It is in parishes like these where strong preaching and liturgy, genuine outreach, and a welcoming community are important values. And they are not alone.

It happens at Holy Trinity in Washington, where justice-oriented preaching and a multi-service outreach packs the Masses every Sunday. More than half the worshipers are coming from Arlington, Virginia, outside the Washington archdiocese.

It happens at parishes like St. Nicholas in Evanston, Illinois, where Massgoers, gathered all around the altar, speak of the profound, often moving sense of community they feel. Says parishioner Joe Boyle, "When the priest lifts up the consecrated bread and wine, I see these holy things amid the faces on the other side of the altar, and it's like I'm linked with all of them and we're all being lifted up."

It occurs in an area of rural Minnesota near Murdock, where five small parishes that were clustered together 24 years ago have developed a sense of community, sharing, and concern for the larger world that surpasses anything that existed when each was independent.

And the Eucharist is working in St. James Cathedral in Seattle, Washington, where the words "I am in your midst as one who serves" appear around a beautiful skylight high over the altar. "I had always thought of liturgy as a place where I could hide and recover from my difficulties," says Bill McJohn, a computer programmer. "But after I moved here and heard the preaching and saw what was going on, like the ministry to the homeless, I finally got it. The liturgy feeds us in order to do the work God sets before us."

Reflection Questions

1. Explain the difference between the weekend as a time of rest and Sunday as a day of rest, as explained in *On Keeping Sunday Holy.*

2. How is the celebration of the Holy Eucharist connected to works of mercy, charity, and apostolic outreach?

3. Examine how your parish, your faith community, or a nearby parish lives the Eucharist and the works it calls us to. Provide examples.

4. Write a brief paragraph explaining how your family and friends could better experience the Sabbath in the manner explained in these two readings.

Endnotes

1. Cf. Codex Iuris Canonici, can. 1247.

6

The Fourth Commandment: "Honor your father and your mother."

The fourth commandment opens the second table of the Decalogue. It shows us the order of charity. God has willed that, after him, we should honor our parents to whom we owe life and who have handed on to us the knowledge of God. We are obliged to honor and respect all those whom God, for our good, has vested with his authority. (*CCC*, no. 2197)

Introduction

When Jesus was asked which law was the greatest (Matthew 22:36–40), he answered by citing the commands to love God (Deuteronomy 6:5) and neighbor (Leviticus 19:18). The *Catechism of the Catholic Church* presents the Ten Commandments in light of Jesus's twofold answer. The first three commandments concern how we are to love God, while the remaining seven address our interactions with other humans. The first of these addressing human interaction is "Honor your father and your mother." To call our parents "neighbors" may be jarring at first. It almost seems too impersonal to call our parents "neighbors" because they play such a major role in our lives. But reconsidering our relationship with our parents in unfamiliar terms may have the benefit of generating new insights and invigorating our moral outlook.

In *On the Role of the Christian Family in the Modern World (Familiaris Consortio),* John Paul II encourages the family to become what it is: a "community of life and love." One of the most important teachings John Paul II stresses is that the family is a "domestic church." By this he means it can be a microcosm of all the Church should be. He is envisioning the family as the foundation of Church and society, the place where love is taught and learned. It nurtures all relationships that bond people together. As such, the family becomes a "school" where people learn how to love and treat their neighbors. The family is to be a place where love is freely given and received. John Paul II calls it "mutual service" where "each gives and receives."

This mutual service is at the heart of the meaning of the fourth commandment and Kathy Saunders' article "Assisted Living: When It's Your Turn to Care for Your Parents." In the Ancient Near East, there was no Social Security to act as a safety net. Only family bonds ensured that the elderly would be cared for after a lifetime of contributing to family and community. Just as parents provided for their child's every need (shelter, clothing, food, and love), so there comes a time when the child must return this care in kind. Having learned love of neighbor in the "school" of the family, the child returns home to practice it. Neighbor love, within or outside the family, is never without its challenges. Saunders' article portrays the stress and strain experienced by family members trying to care for one another. Love is messy and defies simplistic idealizing, but Saunders' examples also reaffirm our hope in the possibility of practicing genuine love in the real world.

It is clear that the command to honor father and mother actually extends to the family as a whole and even beyond. Love of neighbor is learned within the family and first practiced on those nearest, but does not stop there. It creates a network of relationships that highlights mutual responsibilities and binds together a community.

Excerpts from *On the Role of the Christian Family in the Modern World (Familiaris Consortio)*

by Pope John Paul II

Part Two: The Plan of God for Marriage and the Family

. . . The Family, a Communion of Persons

15. In matrimony and in the family a complex of interpersonal relationships is set up—married life, fatherhood and motherhood, filiation and fraternity—through which each human person is introduced into the "human family" and into the "family of God," which is the Church.

Christian marriage and the Christian family build up the Church: for in the family the human person is not only brought into being and progressively introduced by means of education into the human community, but by means of the rebirth of baptism and education in the faith the child is also introduced into God's family, which is the Church.

. . .

Part Three: The Role of the Christian Family

Family, Become What You Are

17. The family finds in the plan of God the Creator and Redeemer not only its identity, what it is, but also its mission, what it can and should do. The role that God calls the family to perform in history derives from what the family is; its role represents the dynamic and existential development of what it is. Each family finds within itself a summons that cannot be ignored, and that specifies both its dignity and its responsibility: family, become what you are.

Accordingly, the family must go back to the "beginning" of God's creative act, if it is to attain self-knowledge and self-realization in accordance with the inner truth not only of what it is but also of what it does in history. And since in God's plan it has been established as an "intimate community of life and love," the family has the mission to become more and more what it is, that is to say, a community of life and love, in an effort that will find fulfillment, as will everything created and redeemed, in the Kingdom of God. Looking at it in such a way as to reach its very roots, we must say that the essence and role of the family are in the final analysis specified by love. Hence the family has the mission to guard, reveal and communicate love, and this is a living reflection of and a real sharing in God's love for humanity and the love of Christ the Lord for the Church His bride.

Every particular task of the family is an expressive and concrete actuation of that fundamental mission. We must therefore go deeper into the unique riches of the family's mission and probe its contents, which are both manifold and unified.

Thus, with love as its point of departure and making constant reference to it, the recent Synod emphasized four general tasks for the family:
1) forming a community of persons;
2) serving life;
3) participating in the development of society;
4) sharing in the life and mission of the Church.

I – Forming a Community of Persons

Love as the Principle and Power of Communion

18. The family, which is founded and given life by love, is a community of persons: of husband and wife, of parents and children, of relatives. Its first task is to live with fidelity the reality of communion in a constant effort to develop an authentic community of persons.

The inner principle of that task, its permanent power and its final goal is love: without love the family is not a community of persons and, in the same way, without love the family cannot live, grow and perfect itself as a community of persons. What I wrote in the Encyclical

Redemptor hominis applies primarily and especially within the family as such: "Man cannot live without love. He remains a being that is incomprehensible for himself, his life is senseless, if love is not revealed to him, if he does not encounter love, if

Redemptor Hominis
John Paul II's first encyclical (1979), arguing that the world's problems require a deeper understanding of the human person and of Christ ("The Redeemer of Man")

he does not experience it and make it his own, if he does not participate intimately in it."

The love between husband and wife and, in a derivatory and broader way, the love between members of the same family—between parents and children, brothers and sisters and relatives and members of the household—is given life and sustenance by an unceasing inner dynamism leading the family to ever deeper and more intense communion, which is the foundation and soul of the community of marriage and the family. . . .

The Broader Communion of the Family

21. Conjugal communion constitutes the foundation on which is built the broader communion of the family, of parents and children, of brothers and sisters with each other, of relatives and other members of the household.

This communion is rooted in the natural bonds of flesh and blood, and grows to its specifically human perfection with the establishment and maturing of the still deeper and richer bonds

conjugal
pertaining to marriage

of the spirit: the love that animates the interpersonal relationships of the different members of the family constitutes the interior strength that shapes and animates the family communion and community.

The Christian family is also called to experience a new and original communion which confirms and perfects natural and human communion. In fact the grace of Jesus Christ, "the first-born among many brethren" is by its nature and interior dynamism "a grace of brotherhood," as St. Thomas Aquinas calls it. The Holy Spirit, who is poured forth in the celebration of the sacraments, is the living source and inexhaustible sustenance of the supernatural communion that gathers believers and links them with Christ and with each other in the unity of the Church of God. The Christian family constitutes a specific revelation and realization of ecclesial communion, and for this reason too it can and should be called "the domestic Church."

> **supernatural**
>
> pertaining to God as opposed to the natural order of creation

All members of the family, each according to his or her own gift, have the grace and responsibility of building, day by day, the communion of persons, making the family "a school of deeper humanity": this happens where there is care and love for the little ones, the sick, the aged; where there is mutual service every day; when there is a sharing of goods, of joys and of sorrows.

A fundamental opportunity for building such a communion is constituted by the educational exchange between parents and children, in which each gives and receives. By means of love, respect and obedience towards their parents, children offer their specific and irreplaceable contribution to the construction of an authentically human and Christian family. They will be aided in this if parents exercise their unrenounceable authority as a true and proper "ministry," that is, as a service to the human and Christian well-being of their children, and in particular as a service aimed at helping them acquire a truly responsible freedom, and if parents maintain a living awareness of the "gift" they continually receive from their children.

Family communion can only be preserved and perfected through a great spirit of sacrifice. It requires, in fact, a ready and generous openness of each and all to understanding, to forbearance, to pardon, to reconciliation. There is no family that does not know how selfishness, discord, tension and conflict violently attack and at times mortally wound its own communion: hence there arise the many and varied forms of division in family life. But, at the same time, every family is called by the God of peace to have the joyous and renewing experience of "reconciliation," that is, communion reestablished, unity restored. In particular, participation in the sacrament of Reconciliation and in the banquet of the one Body of Christ offers to the Christian family the grace and the responsibility of overcoming every division and of moving towards the fullness of communion willed by God, responding in this way to the ardent desire of the Lord: "that they may be one."

Excerpts from *"Assisted Living: When It's Your Turn to Care for Your Parents"*

by Kathy Saunders

Kathy Bingham knew she had reached midlife when she stopped using her sick leave for her children and started using it to care for her mom. Her 83-year-old mother lives on a farm in a rural area about 80 miles from Houston. She still tends to her garden every day and loves to drive her riding mower. She bought a new one last year.

It's not her mother driving the lawn mower that worries Bingham as much as her mother still driving a car.

"That will probably be the next thing we address," she says. Since losing her husband six years ago, Bingham's mother has found a new doctor within 15 miles of her farm. She used to drive 40 miles. Bingham's brother owns the family farm now and helps manage the affairs of his mother and her aging sister, who lives in the same community.

Bingham's family issues, including the looming possibility of having to take her mother's car keys, are what fuels her passion for caregivers. As the director of the Office of Aging for the Archdiocese of Galveston-Houston, Bingham spends her days fielding calls and e-mails from children of aging parents. For almost 30 years her office has been helping parishes establish senior ministry programs. She's been successful in three quarters of the diocese's parishes, offering resources, support, training, conferences, and days of prayer. . . .

"How you treat the most frail is an indicator of how society is going," said Bingham. "These are people who contribute significant amounts of time to their parishes and their parish communities."

The Elderly in the Living Room

Families usually wait way too long to make decisions about their aging parents, says Ethel Sharp of Aging Matters, a St. Petersburg, Florida, nonprofit corporation that helps seniors stay independent as long as possible and offers caregivers support and advice on when older adults should consider assisted living.

hospice
the practice of offering medical, emotional, and spiritual care to a dying person in the patient's home or in an inpatient facility

"The biggest thing I try to do is ward off crisis," says Sharp. "When people are in such a panic, they call all the wrong shots. They think everyone needs to go in a nursing home now, and they don't know their options."

As a teenager in New Rochelle, New York, Sharp watched her mother die of brain cancer. In the days before hospice care, her parents' bedroom was turned into a hospital ward, and the family nursed her mother to the end.

"It was spectacular," says Sharp, describing her mother's grace-filled death and the support of her family. She remembers the prayer vigils at her mother's bedside and the peace that prevailed throughout her illness.

A contributor to the senior section of the St. Petersburg Times, Sharp has worked in aging issues for decades, including for her diocese in Florida. She draws on volumes of experience in her own life. In addition to watching her mother die, she also cared for her mother-in-law until her death.

While her children were still in grade school, Sharp's mother-in-law suffered a paralyzing stroke in New Jersey. Family members up north decided to put her in a nursing home, but Sharp, recalling the peaceful decline of her own mother, insisted she move in with her family instead.

"That's when I really began to understand the nitty grittys and the emotions of caregiving," says Sharp. "My mother-in-law came here resentful that she was even alive with that condition. The more I did, the more she demanded."

Sharp says she never felt so alone. Her friends didn't understand what she was going through. They weren't having to bathe their mothers-in-law or take them to the toilet.

"We talk openly about our babies and our kids. We share birthing stories. But we rarely discuss our aging parents. It's still a disgrace that your perfect mother or father is now unable to speak right or walk right," said Sharp. "In our minds, our parents were the ones with all the answers. The child within us still calls out to mom and dad. It's dreadful to realize that these people who represent our security and togetherness are now incapable."

Sharp, who has counseled thousands of aging adults and their caregivers, believes that's the reason so many children distance themselves from aging parents or let another sibling handle the responsibilities. In many cases she is the one who ends up caring for the seniors referred to her agency. . . .

A Family Affair

Mary Jo Murphy lost her mother, Esther O'Brien, to vascular dementia on Palm Sunday of this year. One of seven children, Murphy and her siblings began caring for her mother while their father, Jack, was dying. Her sister, Rita Rewiski of north Florida, describes the initial realization that her father's health

> **dementia**
> a usually progressive deterioration of mental powers such as memory and judgment

was failing: The strong man who had a penchant for details started becoming too weak to handle daily activities.

Murphy and her brother, Father Michael O'Brien, visited her parents regularly to handle day-to-day tasks. Eventually Rewiski traveled to St. Petersburg once a month to stay with her parents and handle their finances.

"Later Daddy's ability to drive was a problem," she says. After a family discussion and a lot of prayer, Rewiski and her siblings asked her father not to drive until he finished a month of exercise classes to improve his strength and mobility.

"He was never strong enough to attend his classes, so the driving issue just faded away," she says.

Other issues were more problematic. When their mother lost interest in cooking, the family arranged for

Meals-on-Wheels to deliver food. That lasted a year, until their mother called and canceled the service.

"This is when the real difficulty began. They had slowly become more and more private, not wanting outsiders in the house. They didn't want the cleaning lady anymore either. Their personal hygiene changed— they didn't see the need for daily bathing anymore," says Rewiski.

The O'Brien children ultimately gave their parents the choice of hiring help or moving to an assisted-living facility. They reluctantly agreed to hire six caregivers who remained close to the parents and family until Jack O'Brien's death in 2004.

"Watching a parent age, lose abilities, and become completely dependent on others for basic needs is very difficult. In a manner of speaking, I grieved their ultimate loss a little bit at a time with each physical or mental loss," says Rewiski.

By the time her husband died, Esther O'Brien's dementia was obvious. Her children sold her home and moved her to an assisted-living center next door to her son's parish. She stayed there for a year until it was clear her illness had progressed.

At the end of her mother's life, Murphy visited the Clearwater nursing home regularly to help feed her. She recalled one morning when she was feeding her mother breakfast.

"She lost so much weight. I just kept encouraging her to eat. At one point, she stopped opening her mouth for me, looked up and said, 'Who's the mother, you or me?' I assured her that she was still the mother and that I loved her and was trying to encourage her to eat so she would stay well." To Murphy, that exchange epitomized the journey with her mother.

The O'Briens were a faith-filled couple who prayed the rosary every day of their 65-year marriage. Murphy and her own children recited the same prayers at her mother's deathbed. Father O'Brien anointed his mother on Palm Sunday morning and left the nursing home to celebrate Mass at his parish. When the choir sang the words, "Were you there when they crucified my Lord?" O'Brien says he knew that was the moment of his mother's death. At the same moment, Murphy, her husband, son, and sister prayed from a book of Catholic blessings.

"I have new eyes, new understanding, a new way of loving because of experiencing the gradual death of my dear father and mother," says Murphy. "Through all of this I have seen how love has deeply increased in all of us in caring for our mother and father, so I know it is true what Pope John Paul II said about suffering—that it 'is in the world in order to release love.'"

At Home

Father Jean Robitaille, a Missionary of Africa who had to return home from the mission field in 1987 to care for his aging parents, says faith makes the journey possible. "Spiritual people can deal with this more easily because they allow Jesus to guide them in life. They see Jesus as the one in need beside them, and it becomes an act of love."

He compared it to getting up in the middle of the night to feed a baby. "If you are a person who sees that in doing this you are giving God glory and growing closer to the Lord, you can do it." . . .

Before his father, Raoul, died of congestive heart failure in 2000, Robitaille visited twice daily to change his catheter, bathe, and feed him. He purchased a mobile home near his parents in order to be close by. Because his father's mind was intact and because his mother was there to keep him company, Robitaille's 82-year-old dad was able to remain at home until his death. His mother, however, is now in a nursing home.

"I was feeling uncomfortable leaving her alone," says Robitaille. Without her husband's companionship, Germaine Robitaille was declining. When she fell and broke her hip, her son and her doctors determined she needed more care and found an assisted living center. He brought her own chair and photographs to smooth the transition. After another fall, she was moved to a nursing home.

. . .

Dr. Tom Robison, a Catholic general practitioner, helped bathe and shave his father before he died of Alzheimer's disease in 1998. Today, whenever he sees an adult with an aging parent, he treats them both as patients.

Alzheimer's disease
the most common form of dementia

"I think it's a great time as a physician to broach the spiritual aspects of aging," he says.

His own father's death was peaceful, and he was surrounded by family members. But some of his patients struggle as much with family issues as with illness and aging. He referred to one woman who cared for her husband with Alzheimer's for years.

"She hung in so long and finally had to put him in a home where he lasted about six weeks until he died. Her in-laws never spoke to her again. I think what she had been through is nothing less than heroic," he says.

Kathy Bingham in Houston offers retreats for caregivers who suffer such losses. She also puts them in touch with other caregivers who can provide support when families fall apart.

Along with ministering to their caregivers, Bingham provides the seniors themselves with an outlet for their anger or fear or other emotions attached to aging. She conducts workshops about faith-filled aging and looks at ways in which elder adults can pass along their faith to their children and grandchildren.

"For example, our families don't talk about vocations like they did 30 years ago. Maybe these are things seniors can talk about as they go for a walk with their grandchildren. Or they can share the traditions of the holy water font in their parishes," she says.

"With any luck," says Bingham, "we will all grow old."

For Reflection

1. According to *Familiaris Consortio,* what does "honor your mother and father" tell us about our relationship with God? our relationships with other adults? our relationships with the larger community? Support your answers with quotations from the reading.

2. Write a paragraph explaining how you can honor your parents. Provide specific examples from the readings to support your description. Write a paragraph describing how you would like your parents to honor you.

3. Describe the relationship you would like to have with your children when they are your age. What traits do you need to develop to make this happen?

7

The Fifth Commandment: "You shall not murder."

Human life is sacred because from its beginning it involves the creative action of God and it remains for ever in a special relationship with the Creator, who is its sole end. God alone is the Lord of life from its beginning until its end: no one can under any circumstance claim for himself the right directly to destroy an innocent human being.[1] (*CCC*, no. 2258)

Introduction

Imagine that the most popular teacher in your school, the one who has established a rapport with you and your classmates, sets aside the lesson for a day. Rather than discuss your homework or sermonize on the merits of going to college, he tries to persuade you to undertake a great adventure. He promises you not only excitement, but also glory and the admiration of your friends, family, and neighbors. Inspired by notions of patriotism and duty, you and most of your classmates enlist in the army.

This is how Paul Bäumer, the central character of Erich Maria Remarque's *All Quiet on the Western Front*, enters World War I. Trench warfare, poison gas, and machine guns result in high casualties with little or no gain of territory. Surrounded by pointless death and devastation, he and his friends very quickly become disillusioned. They begin to doubt they will even be fit to return to normal life should they survive the war. In the excerpt provided, Paul gets lost at night during a bombardment. No longer sure which direction leads back to his countrymen and which toward the enemy lines, he hides in a shell hole. When the French soldiers make a charge, one of them stumbles over Paul. Terrified, Paul stabs the man and is then forced to remain with this stranger while he slowly dies. Over the next few hours, Paul nears hysteria, and in his frantic thoughts comes to grasp, perhaps for the first time, what Pope John Paul II referred to in *The Gospel of Life (Evangelium Vitae)* as "the incomparable value of every human person."

The encyclical *The Gospel of Life*, promulgated on March 25, 1995, explores the inherent sacredness of all human life. Pope John Paul II was concerned that contemporary life was eroding respect for human dignity. Aside from particular threats such as war, poverty, famine, abortion, and euthanasia, he sensed the advance of a pervasive "culture of death" overly concerned with "efficiency." In such a perspective, some life—because it is inconvenient or requires "greater acceptance"—is regarded as a burden rather than a gift of immeasurable value. Against such currents John Paul II reemphasizes the sacredness of all human life.

The fifth commandment forbids illegal killing of innocent people, but not necessarily war or capital punishment. The Catholic Tradition has developed a just-war theory and recognized the right of states to use the death penalty. *The Gospel of Life,* however, suggests that the death penalty is no longer necessary for the protection of society and is clearly averse to unnecessary war or violence. The thrust of the "gospel of life" is to oppose the "culture of death" in all its forms. The following excerpt from *Evangelium Vitae* concludes that practices opposed to human life do more harm to those who practice them than to those who suffer from them, an assertion seemingly confirmed by the experiences of Paul Bäumer and his comrades.

Excerpt from *The Gospel of Life (Evangelium Vitae)*

by Pope John Paul II

Introduction

1. The Gospel of life is at the heart of Jesus' message. Lovingly received day after day by the Church, it is to be preached with dauntless fidelity as "good news" to the people of every age and culture.

> **fidelity**
> trustworthiness or faithfulness; keeping one's promises

At the dawn of salvation, it is the Birth of a Child which is proclaimed as joyful news: "I bring you good news of a great joy which will come to all the people; for to you is born this day in the city of David a Saviour, who is Christ the Lord" (Lk 2:10–11). The source of this "great joy" is the Birth of the Saviour; but Christmas also reveals the full meaning of every human birth, and the joy which accompanies the Birth of the Messiah is thus seen to be the foundation and fulfilment of joy at every child born into the world (cf. Jn 16:21).

When he presents the heart of his redemptive mission, Jesus says: "I came that they may have life, and have it abundantly" (Jn 10:10). In truth, he is referring to that "new" and "eternal" life which consists in communion with the Father, to which every person is freely called in the Son by the power of the Sanctifying Spirit. It is precisely in this "life" that all the aspects and stages of human life achieve their full significance.

> **redemptive**
> serving to atone for or release from blame

The Incomparable Worth of the Human Person

2. Man is called to a fullness of life which far exceeds the dimensions of his earthly existence, because it consists in sharing the very life of God. The loftiness of this supernatural vocation reveals the greatness and the inestimable value of human life even in its temporal phase. Life in time, in fact, is the fundamental condition, the initial stage and an integral part of the entire unified process of human existence. It is a process which, unexpectedly and

undeservedly, is enlightened by the promise and renewed by the gift of divine life, which will reach its full realization in eternity (cf. 1 Jn 3:1–2). At the same time, it is precisely this supernatural calling which highlights the relative character of each individual's earthly life. After all, life on earth is not an "ultimate" but a "penultimate" reality; even so, it remains a sacred reality entrusted to us, to be preserved with a sense of responsibility and brought to perfection in love and in the gift of ourselves to God and to our brothers and sisters.

> **relative**
> dependent upon other conditions for its proportionate significance; not absolute

> **penultimate**
> next to last

The Church knows that this Gospel of life, which she has received from her Lord, has a profound and persuasive echo in the heart of every person—believer and non-believer alike—because it marvellously fulfils all the heart's expectations while infinitely surpassing them. Even in the midst of difficulties and uncertainties, every person sincerely open to truth and goodness can, by the light of reason and the hidden action of grace, come to recognize in the natural law written in the heart (cf. Rom 2:14–15) the sacred value of human life from its very beginning until its end, and can affirm the right of every human being to have this primary good respected to the highest degree. Upon the recognition of this

> **natural law**
> universal norms of right and wrong that can be known by all through reason

right, every human community and the political community itself are founded.

In a special way, believers in Christ must defend and promote this right, aware as they are of the wonderful truth recalled by the Second Vatican Council: "By his incarnation the Son of God has united himself in some fashion with every human being." This saving event reveals to humanity not only the boundless love of God who "so loved the world that he gave his only Son" (Jn 3:16), but also the incomparable value of every human person.

> **incarnation**
>
> the doctrine that God became "fully human" (while also remaining fully divine) in the person of Jesus

The Church, faithfully contemplating the mystery of the Redemption, acknowledges this value with ever new wonder. She feels called to proclaim to the people of all times this "Gospel," the source of invincible hope and true joy for every period of history. The Gospel of God's love for man, the Gospel of the dignity of the person and the Gospel of life are a single and indivisible Gospel.

For this reason, man—living man—represents the primary and fundamental way for the Church.

New Threats to Human Life

3. Every individual, precisely by reason of the mystery of the Word of God who was made flesh (cf. Jn 1:14), is entrusted to the maternal care of the Church. Therefore every threat to human dignity and life must necessarily be

felt in the Church's very heart; it cannot but affect her at the core of her faith in the Redemptive Incarnation of the Son of God, and engage her in her mission of proclaiming the Gospel of life in all the world and to every creature (cf. Mk 16:15).

Today this proclamation is especially pressing because of the extraordinary increase and gravity of threats to the life of individuals and peoples, especially where life is weak and defenceless. In addition to the ancient scourges of poverty, hunger, endemic diseases, violence and war, new threats are emerging on an alarmingly vast scale.

The Second Vatican Council, in a passage which retains all its relevance today, forcefully condemned a number of crimes and attacks against human life. Thirty years later, taking up the words of the Council and with the same forcefulness I repeat that condemnation in the name of the whole Church, certain that I am interpreting the genuine sentiment of every upright conscience: "Whatever is opposed to life itself, such as any type of murder, genocide, abortion, euthanasia, or wilful self-destruction, whatever violates the integrity of the human person, such as mutilation, torments inflicted on body or mind, attempts to coerce the will itself; whatever insults human dignity, such as subhuman living conditions, arbitrary imprisonment, deportation, slavery, prostitution, the selling of women and children; as well as disgraceful working conditions, where people are treated as mere instruments of gain rather than as free and responsible persons; all these things and others like them are infamies indeed. They poison human society, and they do more

harm to those who practise them than to those who suffer
from the injury. Moreover, they are a supreme dishonour
to the Creator."

Excerpt from *All Quiet on the Western Front*

by Erich Maria Remarque

I lie huddled in a large shell-hole, my legs in the water
up to the belly. When the attack starts I will let myself fall
into the water, with my face as deep in the mud as I can
keep it without suffocating. I must pretend to be dead.

Suddenly I hear the barrage lift. At once I slip down
into the water, my helmet on the nape of my neck and my
mouth just clear so that I can get a breath of air.

I lie motionless;—somewhere something clanks, it
stamps and stumbles nearer—all my nerves become taut
and icy. It clatters over me and away, the first wave has
passed. I have but this one shattering thought: What will
you do if someone jumps into your shell-hole?—Swiftly
I pull out my little dagger, grasp it fast and bury it in my
hand once again under the mud. If anyone jumps in here
I will go for him. It hammers in my forehead; at once, stab
him clean through the throat, so that he cannot call out;
that's the only way; he will be just as frightened as I am;
when in terror we fall upon one another, then I must be
first.

Now our batteries are firing. A shell lands near me. That makes me savage with fury, all it needs now is to be killed by our own shells; I curse and grind my teeth in the mud; it is a raving frenzy; in the end all I can do is groan and pray.

The crash of the shells bursts in my ears. If our fellows make a counter-raid I will be saved. I press my head against the earth and listen to the muffled thunder, like the explosions of quarrying—and raise it again to listen for the sounds on top.

The machine-guns rattle. I know our barbed wire entanglements are strong and almost undamaged;—parts of them are charged with a powerful electric current. The rifle fire increases. They have not broken through; they have to retreat.

I sink down again, huddled, strained to the uttermost. The banging, the creeping, the clanging becomes audible. One single cry yelling amongst it all. They are raked with fire, the attack is repulsed.

*

Already it has become somewhat lighter. Steps hasten over me. The first. Gone. Again, another. The rattle of machine-guns becomes an unbroken chain. Just as I am about to turn round a little, something heavy stumbles, and with a crash a body falls over me into the shell-hole, slips down, and lies across me—

I do not think at all, I make no decision—I strike madly home, and feel only how the body suddenly convulses, then becomes limp, and collapses. When I recover myself, my hand is sticky and wet.

The man gurgles. It sounds to me as though he bellows, every gasping breath is like a cry, a thunder—but it is only my heart pounding. I want to stop his mouth, stuff it with earth, stab him again, he must be quiet, he is betraying me; now at last I regain control of myself, but have suddenly become so feeble that I cannot any more lift my hand against him.

So I crawl away to the farthest corner and stay there, my eyes glued on him, my hand grasping the knife—ready, if he stirs, to spring at him again. But he won't do so any more, I can hear that already in his gurgling.

I can see him indistinctly. I have but one desire, to get away. If it is not soon it will be too light; it will be difficult enough now. Then as I try to raise up my head I see it is impossible already. The machine-gunfire so sweeps the ground that I should be shot through and through before I could make one jump.

I test it once with my helmet, which I take off and hold up to find out the level of the shots. The next moment it is knocked out of my hand by a bullet. The fire is sweeping very low to the ground. I am not far enough from the enemy line to escape being picked off by one of the snipers if I attempt to get away.

comrade

a friend who shares in one's activities, particularly a fellow soldier

The light increases. Burning I wait for our attack. My hands are white at the knuckles, I clench them so tightly in my longing for the fire to cease so that my comrades may come.

Minute after minute trickles away. I dare not look again at the dark figure in the shell-hole. With an effort I look past it and wait, wait. The bullets hiss, they make a steel net, never ceasing, never ceasing.

Then I notice my bloody hand and suddenly feel nauseated. I take some earth and rub the skin with it; now my hand is muddy and the blood cannot be seen any more.

The fire does not diminish. It is equally heavy from both sides. Our fellows have probably given me up for lost long ago.

*

It is early morning, clear and grey. The gurgling continues, I stop my ears, but soon take my fingers away again, because then I cannot hear the other sound.

The figure opposite me moves. I shrink together and involuntarily look at it. Then my eyes remain glued to it. A man with a small pointed beard lies there; his head is fallen to one side, one arm is half-bent, his head rests helplessly upon it. The other hand lies on his chest, it is bloody.

He is dead, I say to myself, he must be dead, he doesn't feel anything any more; it is only the body that is gurgling there. Then the head tries to raise itself, for a moment the groaning becomes louder, his forehead sinks back upon his arm. The man is not dead, he is dying, but he is not dead. I drag myself toward him, hesitate, support myself on my hands, creep a bit farther, wait, again a terrible journey of three yards, a long, a terrible journey. At last I am beside him.

Then he opens his eyes. He must have heard me, for he gazes at me with a look of utter terror. The body lies still, but in the eyes there is such an extraordinary expression of fright that for a moment I think they have power enough to carry the body off with them. Hundreds of miles away with one bound. The body is still perfectly still, without a sound, the gurgle has ceased, but the eyes cry out, yell, all the life is gathered together in them for one tremendous effort to flee, gathered together there in a dreadful terror of death, of me.

My legs give way and I drop on my elbows. "No, no," I whisper.

The eyes follow me. I am powerless to move so long as they are there.

Then his hand slips slowly from his breast, only a little bit, it sinks just a few inches, but this movement breaks the power of the eyes. I bend forward, shake my head and whisper: "No, no, no," I raise one hand, I must show him that I want to help him, I stroke his forehead.

The eyes shrink back as the hand comes, then they lose their stare, the eyelids droop lower, the tension is past. I open his collar and place his head more comfortably.

His mouth stands half open, it tries to form words. The lips are dry. My water bottle is not there. I have not brought it with me. But there is water in the mud, down at the bottom of the crater. I climb down, take out my handkerchief, spread it out, push it under and scoop up the yellow water that strains through into the hollow of my hand.

He gulps it down. I fetch some more. Then I unbutton his tunic in order to bandage him if it is possible. In any case I must do it, so that if the fellows over there capture me they will see that I wanted to help him, and so will not shoot me. He tries to resist, but his hand is too feeble. The shirt is stuck and will not come away, it is buttoned at the back. So there is nothing for it but to cut it open.

I look for the knife and find it again. But when I begin to cut the shirt the eyes open once more and the cry is in them again and the demented expression, so that I must close them, press them shut and whisper: "I want to help you, Comrade, camerade, camerade, camerade—" eagerly repeating the word, to make him understand.

field dressing
bandages an ordinary soldier would carry

There are three stabs. My field dressing covers them, the blood runs out under it, I press it tighter; there; he groans.

That is all I can do. Now we must wait, wait.

*

These hours. . . . The gurgling starts again—but how slowly a man dies! For this I know—he cannot be saved, I have, indeed, tried to tell myself that he will be, but at noon this pretence breaks down and melts before his groans. If only I had not lost my revolver crawling about, I would shoot him. Stab him I cannot.

pretence
a false appearance or implication

By noon I am groping on the outer limits of reason. Hunger devours me, I could almost weep for something to eat, I cannot struggle against it. Again and again I fetch water for the dying man and drink some myself.

This is the first time I have killed with my hands, whom I can see close at hand, whose death is my doing. Kat and Kropp and Müller have experienced it already, when they have hit someone; it happens to many, in hand-to-hand fighting especially—

But every gasp lays my heart bare. This dying man has time with him, he has an invisible dagger with which he stabs me: Time and my thoughts.

I would give much if he would but stay alive. It is hard to lie here and to have to see and hear him.

In the afternoon, about three, he is dead.

I breathe freely again. But only for a short time. Soon the silence is more unbearable than the groans. I wish the gurgling were there again, gasping, hoarse, now whistling softly and again hoarse and loud.

It is mad, what I do. But I must do something. I prop the dead man up again so that he lies comfortably, al-though he feels nothing any more. I close his eyes. They are brown, his hair is black and a bit curly at the sides.

The mouth is full and soft beneath his moustache; the nose is slightly arched, the skin brownish; it is now not so pale as it was before, when he was still alive. For a mo-ment the face seems almost healthy;—then it collapses suddenly into the strange face of the dead that I have so often seen, strange faces, all alike.

No doubt his wife still thinks of him; she does not know what has happened. He looks as if he would have often have [sic]written to her;—she will still be getting mail from him—To-morrow, in a week's time—perhaps even a stray letter a month hence. She will read it, and in it he will be speaking to her.

My state is getting worse, I can no longer control my thoughts. What would his wife look like? Like the little brunette on the other side of the canal? Does she belong to me now? Perhaps by this act she becomes mine. I wish Kantorek were sitting here beside me. If my mother could see me—. The dead man might have had thirty more years of life if only I had impressed the way back to our trench more sharply on my memory. If only he had run two yards farther to the left, he might now be sitting in the trench over there and writing a fresh letter to his wife.

But I will get no further that way; for that is the fate of all of us: if Kemmerich's leg had been six inches to the right: if Haie Westhus had bent his back three inches further forward—

*

The silence spreads. I talk and must talk. So I speak to him and say to him: "Comrade, I did not want to kill you. If you jumped in here again, I would not do it, if you would be sensible too. But you were only an idea to me before, an abstraction that lived in my mind and called forth its appropriate response. It was that abstraction I stabbed. But now, for the first time, I see you are a man like me. I thought of your hand-grenades, of your bayonet, of your rifle; now I see your wife and your face and our fellowship. Forgive me, comrade. We always see it too late. Why do they never tell us that you are poor devils like us, that your mothers are just as anxious as ours, and that we have the same fear of death, and the same dying and the same agony—Forgive me, comrade; how could you be my enemy? If we threw away these rifles and this uniform you could be my brother just like Kat and Albert. Take twenty years of my life, comrade, and stand up—take more, for I do not know what I can even attempt to do with it now."

It is quiet, the front is still except for the crackle of rifle fire. The bullets rain over, they are not fired haphazard, but shrewdly aimed from all sides. I cannot get out.

"I will write to your wife," I say hastily to the dead man, "I will write to her, she must hear it from me, I will tell her everything I have told you, she shall not suffer, I will help her, and your parents too, and your child—"

His tunic is half open. The pocket-book is easy to find. But I hesitate to open it. In it is the book with his name. So long as I do not know his name perhaps I may still forget him, time will obliterate it, this picture. But his name, it is a nail that will be hammered into me and never come out again. It has the power to recall this for ever, it will always come back and stand before me.

irresolutely
indecisively; lacking confidence; in a way that is unsure of how to proceed

Irresolutely I take the wallet in my hand. It slips out of my hand and falls open. Some pictures and letters drop out. I gather them up and want to put them back again, but the strain I am under, the uncertainty, the hunger, the danger, these hours with the dead man have made me desperate, I want to hasten the relief, to intensify and to end the torture, as one strikes an unendurably painful hand against the trunk of a tree, regardless of everything.

There are portraits of a woman and a little girl, small amateur photographs taken against an ivy-clad wall. Along with them are letters. I take them out and try to read them. Most of it I do not understand, it is so hard to decipher and I scarcely know any French. But each word I translate pierces me like a shot in the chest;—like a stab in the chest.

My brain is taxed beyond endurance. But I realize this much, that I will never dare to write to these people as I intended. Impossible. I look at the portraits once more; they are clearly not rich people. I might send them money anonymously if I earn anything later on. I seize upon that, it is at least something to hold on to. This dead man is bound up with my life, therefore I must do everything, promise every-

> **stratagem**
> a tactic for deceiving an enemy

> **compositor**
> someone who sets type or text for printing

thing in order to save myself; I swear blindly that I mean to live only for his sake and his family, with wet lips I try to placate him—and deep down in me lies the hope that I may buy myself off in this way and perhaps even get out of this; it is a little stratagem: if only I am allowed to escape, then I will see to it. So I open the book and read slowly:—Gérard Duval, compositor.

With the dead man's pencil I write the address on an envelope, then swiftly thrust everything back into his tunic.

I have killed the printer, Gérard Duval. I must be a printer, I think confusedly, be a printer, printer—

For Reflection

1. Provide examples from the excerpt of how Paul Bäumer, in *All Quiet on the Western Front,* begins to identify with the man he has killed.

2. Who are the people impacted by the death of the man in *All Quiet on the Western Front?* Select a current threat to human life in our society and identify the people affected by it.

3. What are current challenges to the sacredness of life and the dignity of the human person in our society? Review a major newspaper and identify two stories that deal with the sacredness of life and the dignity of the human person. Provide specific examples from *The Gospel of Life* explaining your choices.

Endnotes

1. Congregation for the Doctrine of the Faith, instruction, *Donum vitae*, intro. 5.

8

The Sixth Commandment: "You shall not commit adultery."

Chastity means the successful integration of sexuality within the person and thus the inner unity of man in his bodily and spiritual being. Sexuality, in which man's belonging to the bodily and biological world is expressed, becomes personal and truly human when it is integrated into the relationship of one person to another, in the complete and lifelong mutual gift of a man and a woman. (*CCC*, no. 2337)

Introduction

The only way to understand the prohibition of adultery is to explore the deeper meaning of marriage, family, and human sexuality. The foundation for this examination is human nature. In his Letter to Families, John Paul II says it is the Church's job to teach us the truth about ourselves: that we only find ourselves "through a sincere gift of self." The implication is that human beings are social animals, incomplete on their own and made to give themselves away. Because human beings can neither reproduce with-

138

out a partner nor find fulfillment in isolation, marriage is an institution and relationship in which this "gift of self" finds expression, and it is the one the Pope has chosen to focus on in this letter.

The Church views marriage as permanent and exclusive. This is the only way the husband and wife's mutual gift of self can come to full fruition. Otherwise, as Ronald Rolheiser explains in the second reading, a partner holds something back and the gift is not really given. When husband and wife give themselves to each other, it enables deeper intimacy and fulfillment, but also exposes each to a risk. They have made themselves vulnerable, and the marriage vows are a commitment to honor and protect that vulnerability. So the commandment forbids adultery in order to preserve the possibility of a true gift of self.

The gift of self does not just end there, John Paul II asserts, but often leads to the gift of new life in the birth of a child. The parents both receive the gift of the child and, in turn, give themselves away all over again to the child. The commandment, therefore, is also intended to ensure a stable and loving environment for a child.

In *The Holy Longing*, Ronald Rolheiser agrees that sexuality "is about overcoming separateness by giving life and blessing it." One of the merits of the following excerpt is that he provides a number of examples of mature expressions of human sexuality. Images of sexuality in our culture tend to narrow our perception of it to the mechanics of sexual intercourse. Rolheiser's examples have the virtue of expanding our sense of what a healthy sexuality looks like.

Within this broadened vision of sexuality, Rolheiser still insists there are some necessary boundaries. The guidelines he elaborates are largely consistent with John Paul II's vision. He emphasizes sexuality's "sanctity" and its tie to the permanent and exclusive commitment of marriage. Moreover, he illustrates how, through parenthood, sexuality leads to holiness by gradually teaching selflessness and drawing the individual into community with others. Finally, Rolheiser explores the necessity of chastity, but carefully distinguishes it from celibacy.

Excerpt from Letter to Families

by Pope John Paul II

The Sincere Gift of Self

11. After affirming that man is the only creature on earth which God willed for itself, the Council immediately goes on to say that he cannot *"fully find himself except through a sincere gift of self."* This might appear to be a contradiction, but in fact it is not. Instead it is the magnificent paradox of

> **paradox**
> an apparent contradiction that is actually profoundly true

human existence: an existence called *to serve the truth in love.* Love causes man to find fulfilment through the sincere gift of self. To love means to give and to receive something which can be neither bought nor sold, but only given freely and mutually.

By its very nature the gift of the person must be lasting and irrevocable. The indissolubility of marriage flows in the first place from the very essence of that gift: *the gift of one person to another person*. This reciprocal giving of self reveals the *spousal nature of love*. In their marital consent the bride and groom call each other by name: *"I . . . take you . . .* as my wife (as my husband) and I promise to be true to you . . . for all the days of my life." A gift such as this involves an obligation much more serious and profound than anything

> **irrevocable**
> unable to be taken back or recalled

> **indissolubility**
> incapable of being undone; always binding; the idea that marriage is permanent and cannot be undone

which might be "purchased" in any way and at any price. Kneeling before the Father, from whom all fatherhood and motherhood come, the future parents come to realize that they have been "redeemed." They have been purchased at great cost, *by the price* of the most sincere gift of all, *the blood of Christ* of which they partake through the Sacrament. The liturgical crowning of the marriage rite is the Eucharist, the sacrifice of that

> **redeemed**
> bought back; atoned for; released from blame or duty to repay

"Body which has been given up" and that "Blood which has been shed," which in a certain way finds expression in the consent of the spouses.

When a man and woman in marriage mutually give and receive each other in the unity of "one flesh," the logic of the sincere gift of self becomes a part of their life. Without this, marriage would be empty; whereas a communion of persons, built on this logic, becomes a communion of parents. When they transmit *life to the child, a new human "thou" becomes a part of the horizon of the "we" of the spouses,* a person whom they will call by a new name: "our son

conception

the act of becoming pregnant; origin or beginning

. . . ; our daughter . . ." "I have gotten a man with the help of the Lord" (*Gen* 4:1), says Eve, the first woman of history: a human being, first expected for nine months and then "revealed" to parents, brothers and sisters. The process from conception and growth in the mother's womb to birth makes it possible to create a space within which the new creature can be revealed as a "gift": indeed this is what it is from the very beginning. Could this frail and helpless being, totally dependent upon its parents and completely entrusted to them, be seen in any other way? The newborn child gives itself to its parents by the very fact of its coming into existence. *Its existence is already a gift, the first gift of the Creator to the creature.*

In the newborn child is realized the common good of the family. Just as the common good of spouses is fulfilled in conjugal love, ever ready to give and receive new life, so too the common good of the family is fulfilled through that same spousal love, as embodied in the newborn child. Part of the genealogy of the person is the genealogy of the family, preserved for posterity by the annotations in the Church's baptismal registers, even though these are merely the social consequence of the fact that "a man has been born into the world" (cf. *Jn* 16:21).

But is it really true that the new human being is a gift for his parents? A gift for society? Apparently nothing seems to indicate this. On occasion the birth of a child appears to be a simple statistical fact, registered like so many other data in demographic records. It is true that for the parents the birth of a child means more work, new financial burdens and further inconveniences, all of which can lead to the temptation not to want another birth. In some social and cultural contexts this temptation can become very strong. Does this mean that a child is not a gift? That it comes into the world only to take and not to give? These are some of the disturbing questions which men and women today find hard to escape. *A child comes to take up room, when it seems that there is less and less room in the world.* But is it really true that a child brings nothing to the family and society? Is not every child a "particle" of that common good without which human communities break down and risk extinction? Could this ever really be denied? The child becomes a gift to its brothers, sisters, parents and entire family. *Its life becomes a gift for the very people who were givers of life* and who cannot help but feel its presence, its sharing in their life and its contribution to their

> **common good**
> benefits shared by all persons who are members of a family or community (rooted in the belief that human nature is inherently social)

common good and to that of the community of the family. This truth is obvious in its simplicity and profundity, whatever the complexity and even the possible pathology of the psychological make-up of certain persons. *The common good of the whole of society dwells in man;* he is, as we recalled, "the way of the Church." Man is first of all the "glory of God": *"Gloria Dei vivens homo,"* in the celebrated words of Saint Irenaeus, which might also be translated: "the glory of God is for man to be alive." It could be said that here we encounter the loftiest definition of man: *the glory of God is the common good of all that exists;* the common good of the human race.

Saint Irenaeus
second-century Greek bishop and theologian who defended the inclusion of all four Gospels as divinely inspired

Yes! *Man is a common good:* a common good of the family and of humanity, of individual groups and of different communities. But there are significant distinctions of degree and modality in this regard. Man is a common good, for example, of the Nation to which he belongs and of the State of which he is a citizen; but in a much more concrete, unique and unrepeatable way he is a common good of his family. He is such not only as an individual who is part of the multitude of humanity, but rather as *"this individual."* God the Creator calls him into existence "for himself"; and in coming into the world he begins, in the family, his "great adventure," the adventure of human life. "This man" has, in every instance, *the right to fulfil himself on the basis of his human dignity.* It is precisely this dignity which establishes a person's place among others, and above all, in the family. The family is indeed— more than any other human reality— the place where an individual can exist "for himself" through the sincere gift of self. This is why it remains a social institution which neither can nor should be replaced: it is the "sanctuary of life."

The fact that a child is being born, that "a child is born into the world" (Jn 16:21) is a *paschal sign*. As we read in the Gospel of John, Jesus himself speaks of this to the disciples before his passion and death, comparing their sadness at his departure with the pains of a woman in labour: *"When a woman is in travail she has sorrow* (that is, she suffers), because *her hour* has come; but when she is delivered of the child, she no longer remembers the anguish, for *joy that a child is born into the world"* (Jn 16:21). The "hour" of Christ's death (cf. Jn 13:1) is compared here to the "hour" of the woman in birthpangs; the birth of a new child fully reflects the victory of life over death brought about by the Lord's Resurrection. This comparison can provide us with material for reflection. Just as the Resurrection of Christ is the manifestation of *Life* beyond the threshold of death, so too the birth of an infant is a manifestation of life, which is always destined, through Christ, for that *"fullness of life" which is in God himself:* "I came that they may have life, and have it abundantly" (Jn 10:10). Here we see revealed

> **paschal**
> from the Hebrew word for Passover (*pesach*), pertaining to Passover or Easter

the deepest meaning of Saint Irenaeus's expression: *"Gloria Dei vivens homo."*

It is the Gospel truth concerning the gift of self, without which the person cannot "fully find himself," which makes possible an appreciation of how profoundly this "sincere gift" is rooted in the gift of God, Creator and Redeemer, and in the "grace of the Holy Spirit" which the celebrant during the Rite of Marriage prays will be "poured out" on the spouses. Without such an "outpouring," it would be very difficult to understand all this and to carry it out as man's vocation. Yet how many people understand this intuitively! Many men and women make this truth their own, coming to discern that only in this truth do they encounter "the Truth and the Life" (*Jn* 14:6). *Without this truth, the life of the spouses and of the family will not succeed in attaining a fully human meaning.*

This is why the Church never tires of teaching and of bearing witness to this truth. While certainly showing maternal understanding for the many complex crisis situations in which families are involved, as well as for the moral frailty of every human being, the Church is convinced that she must remain absolutely faithful to the truth about human love. Otherwise she would betray herself. To move away from this saving truth would be to close "the eyes of our hearts" (cf. *Eph* 1:18), which instead should always stay open to the light which the Gospel sheds on human affairs (cf. *2 Tim* 1:10). An awareness of that sincere gift of self whereby man "finds himself" must be constantly renewed and safeguarded in the face of the serious opposition which the Church meets on the part of those who advocate a false civilization of progress. The family always expresses a new dimension of good for mankind, and it thus creates a new responsibility. We are speaking of the *responsibility for that particular common good* in which is included the good of the person, of every member of the family community. While certainly a "difficult" good (*"bonum arduum"*), it is also an attractive one.

Excerpts from *The Holy Longing: The Search for a Christian Spirituality*

by Ronald Rolheiser

3. A Christian Definition of Sexuality

How then might a Christian define sexuality? Sexuality is a beautiful, good, extremely powerful, sacred energy, given us by God and experienced in every cell of our being as an irrepressible urge to overcome our incompleteness, to move toward unity and consummation with that which is beyond us. It is also the pulse to celebrate, to give and to receive delight, to find our way back to the Garden of Eden where we can be naked, shameless, and without worry and work as we make love in the moonlight.

Ultimately, though, all these hungers, in their full maturity culminate in one thing: They want to make us co-creators with God . . . mothers and fathers, artisans and creators, big brothers and big sisters, nurses and healers, teachers and consolers, farmers and producers, administrators and community builders . . . co-responsible with

God for the planet, standing with God and smiling at and blessing the world.

Given that definition, we see that sexuality in its mature bloom does not necessarily look like the love scenes (perfect bodies, perfect emotion, perfect light) in a Hollywood movie. What does sexuality in its full bloom look like?

- When you see a young mother, so beaming with delight at her own child that, for that moment, all selfishness within her has given way to the sheer joy of seeing her child happy, you are seeing sexuality in its mature bloom.
- When you see a grandfather so proud of his grandson, who has just received his diploma, that, for that moment, his spirit is only compassion, altruism, and joy, you are seeing sexuality in its mature bloom.
- When you see an artist, after long frustration, look with such satisfaction on a work she has just completed that everything else for the moment is blotted out, you are seeing sexuality in its mature bloom.
- When you see a young man, cold and wet, but happy to have been of service, standing on a dock where he has carried the unconscious body of a child he has just saved from drowning, you are seeing sexuality in its mature bloom.
- When you see someone throw back his or her head in genuine laughter, caught off guard by the surprise of joy itself, you are seeing sexuality in its mature bloom.
- When you see an elderly nun who, never having slept with a man, been married, or given birth to a child, has through years of selfless service become a person whose very compassion gives her a mischievous smile, you are seeing sexuality in its mature bloom.

- When you see a community gathered round a grave, making peace with tragedy and consoling each other so that life can go on, you are seeing sexuality in its mature bloom.
- When you see an elderly husband and wife who after nearly half a century of marriage have made such peace with each other's humanity that now they can quietly share a bowl of soup, content just to know that the other is there, you are seeing sexuality in its mature bloom.
- When you see a table, surrounded by a family, laughing, arguing, and sharing life with each other, you are seeing sexuality in its mature bloom.
- When you see a Mother Teresa dress the wounds of a street-person in Calcutta or an Oscar Romero give his life in defense of the poor, you are seeing sexuality in its mature bloom.
- When you see any person—man, woman, or child—who in a moment of service, affection, love, friendship, creativity, joy, or compassion is, for that moment, so caught up in what is beyond him or her that for that instant his or her separateness from others is overcome, you are seeing sexuality in its mature bloom.
- When you see God, having just created the earth or just seen Jesus baptized in the Jordan river, look down on what has just happened and say, "It is good. In this I take delight!" you are seeing sexuality in its mature bloom.

Sexuality is not simply about finding a lover or even finding a friend. It is about overcoming separateness by giving life and blessing it. Thus, in its maturity, sexuality is about giving oneself over to community, friendship, family, service, creativity, humor, delight, and martyrdom so that, with God, we can help bring life into the world.

4. A Few Nonnegotiable Christian Principles

Beyond the wide definition just given, what other principles anchor a healthy Christian spirituality of sexuality?

Four fundamental principles need special mentioning:

a. For a Christian, sex is something sacred. Hence it can never be simply a casual, unimportant, neutral thing. If its proper nature is respected, it builds the soul as a sacrament, and brings God's physical touch to us. Conversely, though, if its proper nature is not respected, it becomes a perverse thing that works at disintegrating the soul.

In a committed, loving, covenantal relationship sex is sacramental, part of a couple's Eucharist. It is then a privileged vehicle of grace, an extraordinary source of integration for the soul, a deep well of gratitude, and something that will through its own inner dynamics open both persons (in a way that perhaps nothing else can) to becoming life-giving, gracious, and blessing adults. Conversely, sex that is devoid of those conditions will normally bring about the opposite effect. It will harden the soul, trivialize it, and work at disintegrating its unity. It will, as well, not open those engaging in it to real community, graciousness, and blessing, but instead help alienate them from real community. . . .

b. For a Christian, sex by its very nature must be linked to marriage, monogamy, and a covenantal commitment that is, by definition, all-embracing and permanent. What is wrong with sex outside of marriage, for a Christian, is not so much that it breaks a commandment (although it does) but that, ultimately, it is a schizophrenic act. How so?

By its very nature, sex speaks of total giving, total trust, and total commitment. There is an unconditionality inherent in so intimate a sharing of one's soul. Thus, if real trust, commitment, permanency, and unconditionality are not present within the wider relationship, sex is partly a lie. It pretends to give a gift that it does not really give and it asks for a gift that it cannot respectfully reciprocate. When one says, as does an old song, "Let the devil take tomorrow, tonight I need a friend," the devil indeed does take tomorrow and the friend usually disappears as well.

. . .

c. Sex has an inner dynamic that, if followed faithfully, will lead its partners to sanctity. Sexuality is God's energy within us. Hence, ideally, sex should lead persons to sanctity and when its principles are respected it does precisely that. How? What

> **sanctity**
> holiness or inviolability

are its inner dynamics that can lead one to sanctity? Let us look at a typical example:

A young man, nursing more than his share of selfishness, hurt, and personal ambition, sets out to make his mark in life when his sexuality intercepts him. Initially, given the adolescent stage of his development, what he wants is sex, with or without love and intimacy. But he meets a young woman with whom he falls in love. He still wants sex, but now the very inner dynamics of sex help mature his desire. Being in love, his sexuality now demands not just sex but intimacy, exclusivity, and commitment as well. He marries and, for a while, he is satisfied with sex and intimacy. However, as he and his relationship to his wife mature, there naturally comes a day when he wants children. They begin to have children and even though he had wanted them he is surprised at himself by how much he loves his children and how much they have changed him and his whole outlook on life. Whole new dimensions of desire (of which he was previously unaware) are triggered within him and he finds that he can, without resentment, put his own needs aside so as to give more of himself to his children and, of course, to his wife as well.

And then the children start growing up, mixing with other children, going to school, and demanding lessons of every kind. His house starts filling with other children and their parents and their concerns—and he finds himself busy each evening discussing concerns with other parents, attending parent-teacher meetings, coaching kids' football, and driving kids to every kind of class and tournament in the area. His world keeps widening and he, and his desires and maturity, keep widening with it. Slowly, imperceptibly, through the years he grows, widens, mellows out, becomes more unselfish, and a gracious, blessing, adult father.

Sex, followed in fidelity, leads to sanctity. This man's story is one kind of scenario. There are many, many others that work in the same way, including the dynamics of a healthy celibate sexuality. Desire, working through us, if followed faithfully, keeps opening us up further and further to gracious adulthood.[3]

d. For a Christian, sex always needs the protection of a healthy chastity. In the Christian view of things, chastity is one of the keys to a healthy sexuality. This, however, needs to be correctly understood.

First, there is the concept of chastity itself: Chastity is not the same thing as celibacy. To be chaste does not mean that one does not have sex. Nor does it mean that one is a prude. My parents were two of the most chaste persons I ever met, yet they obviously enjoyed sex—as a large family and a warm,

celibacy
remaining unmarried and abstaining from all sexual relationships

vivacious bond between them gave more than ample evidence of. Chastity is, first of all, not even primarily a sexual concept, though, given the power and urgency of sex, faults in chastity are often within the area of sexuality.

Chastity has to do with all experiencing. It is about the appropriateness of any experience. Ultimately, chastity is reverence—and sin, all sin, is irreverence. To be chaste is to experience people, things, places, entertainment, the phases of our lives, and sex in a way that does not violate them or ourselves. To be chaste is to experience things reverently, in such a way that the experience leaves both them and ourselves more, not less, integrated.

For Reflection

1. From your own experience, why are families important? Summarize the reasons families are important according to John Paul II's Letter to Families.

2. Why, according to John Paul II, is physical intimacy essential to a Christian marriage?

3. Who in your life do you witness living sexuality the way Rolheiser describes it? Provide specific examples and explanations.

4. According to Rolheiser, there are a "few nonnegotiable Christian principles." Summarize these principles in your own words.

9

The Seventh Commandment: "You shall not steal."

The seventh commandment forbids unjustly taking or keeping the goods of one's neighbor and wronging him in any way with respect to his goods. It commands justice and charity in the care of earthly goods and the fruits of men's labor. For the sake of the common good, it requires respect for the universal destination of goods and respect for the right to private property. Christian life strives to order this world's goods to God and to fraternal charity. (*CCC*, no. 2401)

Introduction

Increasingly concerned that the U.S. economy could not meet the demands of social justice for all its citizens, in 1986 the National Conference of Catholic Bishops released *Economic Justice for All: Pastoral Letter on Catholic Social Teaching and the U.S. Economy*. Building on the major themes of Catholic social teaching, the bishops detailed the implications of Christian faith for social and economic life. At the center is the human person, who has a sacred dignity. This dignity is neither gained nor lost through individual merit; it comes with being created in the image of God. As we saw in the last chapter, the Church views human nature as essentially social and fulfilled only in community. Therefore, from a Catholic perspective, a just economic system must sustain a community of solidarity that promotes human dignity for every member.

In the selected excerpt from the bishops' letter, it is explained that the sacred dignity of the human person shapes the definitions of commutative, distributive, and social justice. Commutative justice is the standard that regulates exchanges between parties; for example, commutative justice prohibits cheating a partner in a business exchange. Distributive justice demands that the basic needs of every person be met. This means that no one has the "right" to own more than needed, to the detriment of another. Social justice addresses the common rights and duties of individuals and groups to participate in society. For instance, each person is entitled to a safe and properly compensated job in order to provide for the needs of life and family. Correspondingly, each person has an obligation to contribute to the common good of others. In all three—commutative, distributive, and social justice—the good of the community is interwoven and balanced with the needs of the individual.

In relation to the commandment addressing stealing, all three forms of justice are integral. It is a form of stealing when someone acts dishonestly in a business transaction. It is stealing when an employer does not pay a just wage to an employee. Stealing is more than just taking something from someone else—it is denying someone else's needs for the sake of greed or pride. Stealing, then, cannot be understood apart from justice and human dignity.

The first reading concludes with the bishops' directive that "all of us must examine our way of living in light of the needs of the poor." In the second reading, Matthew McGarry examines his "way of living" in the broader context of the needs of the international community. Working with Catholic Relief Services, he is under no illusion that he can save the world, nor is he so arrogant as to assume he knows how to "fix" the lives of the poor in Darfur. In fact, he is humble enough to learn from them, as in the example of his friendship with Mohamed. The story of McGarry's service and Mohamed's work shows two ways to fulfill the right and obligation to participate in community that constitute social justice. This notion of participation illustrates that observing the seventh commandment is not merely a matter of refraining from theft; it also involves the active duty to give.

Excerpt from *Economic Justice for All: Pastoral Letter on Catholic Social Teaching and the U.S. Economy*

by the United States Conference of Catholic Bishops

1. The Responsibilities of Social Living

63. Human life is life in community. Catholic social teaching proposes several complementary perspectives that show how moral responsibilities and duties in the economic sphere are rooted in this call to community.

a. Love and Solidarity

64. *The commandments to love God with all one's heart and to love one's neighbor as oneself are the heart and soul of Christian morality.* Jesus offers himself as the model of this all-inclusive love: ". . . love one another as I have loved you" (Jn 15:12). These commands point out the path toward true human fulfillment and happiness. They are not arbitrary restrictions on human freedom. Only active love of God and neighbor makes the fullness of community happen. Christians look forward in hope to a true communion among all persons with each other and with God. The Spirit of Christ labors in history to build up the bonds of solidarity among all persons until that day on which their union is brought to perfection in the Kingdom of God.[1] Indeed Christian theological reflection on the very reality of God as a trinitarian unity of persons—Father, Son, and Holy Spirit—shows that being a person means being united to other persons in mutual love."[2]

> **arbitrary**
> depending on chance or whim rather than on good reason

> **trinitarian**
> pertaining to three-in-one

65. What the Bible and Christian tradition teach, human wisdom confirms. Centuries before Christ, the Greeks and Romans spoke of the human person as a "social animal" made for friendship, community, and public life. These insights show that human beings achieve self-realization not in isolation, but in interaction with others.[3]

> **commonweal**
> the common good or public welfare

66. The virtues of citizenship are an expression of Christian love more crucial in today's interdependent world than ever before. These virtues grow out of a lively sense of one's dependence on the commonweal and obligations to it. This civic commitment must also guide the economic institutions of society. In the absence of a vital sense of citizenship among the businesses, corporations, labor unions, and other groups that shape economic life, society as a whole is endangered. Solidarity is another name for this social friendship and civic commitment that make human moral and economic life possible.

> **solidarity**
> unity of feeling, interest, and purpose among people, which promotes justice

67. The Christian tradition recognizes, of course, that the fullness of love and community will be achieved only when God's work in Christ comes to completion in the kingdom of God. This kingdom has been inaugurated among us, but God's redeeming and transforming work is not yet complete. Within history, knowledge of how to achieve the goal of social unity is limited.

Human sin continues to wound the lives of both individuals and larger social bodies and places obstacles in the path toward greater social solidarity. If efforts to protect human dignity are to be effective, they must take these limits on knowledge and love into account. Nevertheless, sober realism should not be confused with resigned or cynical pessimism. It is a challenge to develop a courageous hope that can sustain efforts that will sometimes be arduous and protracted.

b. Justice and Participation

68. Biblical justice is the goal we strive for. This rich biblical understanding portrays a just society as one marked by the fullness of love, compassion, holiness, and peace. On their path through history, however, sinful human beings need more specific guidance on how to move toward the realization of this great vision of God's Kingdom. This guidance is contained in the norms of basic or minimal justice. These norms state the *minimum* levels of mutual care and respect that all persons owe to each other in an imperfect world.[4] Catholic social teaching, like much philosophical reflection, distinguishes three dimensions of basic justice: commutative justice, distributive justice, and social justice.[5]

69. *Commutative justice calls for fundamental fairness in all agreements and exchanges between individuals or private social groups.* It demands respect for the equal human dignity of all persons in economic transactions, contracts, or promises. For example, workers owe their employers diligent work in exchange for their wages. Em-

ployers are obligated to treat their employees as persons, paying them fair wages in exchange for the work done and establishing conditions and patterns of work that are truly human.[6]

70. *Distributive justice requires that the allocation of income, wealth, and power in society be evaluated in light of its effects on persons whose basic material needs are unmet.* The Second Vatican Council stated: "The right to have a share of earthly goods sufficient for oneself and one's family belongs to everyone. The fathers and doctors of the Church held this view, teaching that we are obliged to come to the relief of the poor and to do so not merely out of our superfluous goods."[7] Minimum material resources are an absolute necessity for human life. If persons are to be recognized as members of the human community, then the community has an obligation to help fulfill these basic needs unless an absolute scarcity of resources makes this strictly impossible. No such scarcity exists in the United States today.

> **Second Vatican Council**
> twenty-first ecumenical council of the Roman Catholic Church, opened by Pope John XXIII in 1962 and closed by Pope Paul VI in 1965, which brought about dramatic renewals in liturgy, theology, and ethics

71. *Justice also has implications for the way the larger social, economic, and political institutions of society are organized. Social justice implies that persons have an obligation to be active and productive participants in*

the life of society and that society has a duty to enable them to participate in this way. This form of justice can also be called "contributive," for it stresses the duty of all who are able to help create the goods, services, and other nonmaterial or spiritual values necessary for the welfare of the whole community. In the words of Pius XI, "It is of the very essence of social justice to demand from each individual all that is necessary for the common good."[8] Productivity is essential if the community is to have the resources to serve the well-being of all. Productivity, however, cannot be measured solely by its output in goods and services. Patterns of production must also be measured in light of their impact on the fulfillment of basic needs, employment levels, patterns of discrimination, environmental quality, and sense of community.

72. The meaning of social justice also includes a duty to organize economic and social institutions so that people can contribute to society in ways that respect their freedom and the dignity of their labor. Work should enable the working person to become "more a human being," more capable of acting intelligently, freely, and in ways that lead to self-realization.[9]

73. Economic conditions that leave large numbers of able people unemployed, underemployed, or employed in dehumanizing conditions fail to meet the converging demands of these three forms of basic justice. Work with adequate pay for all who seek it is the primary means for achieving basic justice in our society. Discrimination in job

affirmative action
policy to redress historical inequalities by actively hiring underrepresented peoples

opportunities or income levels on the basis of race, sex, or other arbitrary standards can never be justified.[10] It is a scandal that such discrimination continues in the United States today. Where the effects of past discrimination persist, society has the obligation to take positive steps to overcome the legacy of injustice. Judiciously administered affirmative action programs in education and employment can be important expressions of the drive for solidarity and participation that is at the heart of true justice. Social harm calls for social relief.

74. Basic justice also calls for the establishment of a floor of material well-being on which all can stand. This is a duty of the whole of society and it creates particular obligations for those with greater resources. This duty calls into question extreme inequalities of income and consumption when so many lack basic necessities. Catholic social teaching does not maintain that a flat, arithmetical equality of income and wealth is a demand of justice, but it does challenge economic arrangements that leave large numbers of people impoverished. Further, it sees extreme inequality as a threat to the solidarity of the human community, for great disparities lead to deep social divisions and conflict.[11]

75. This means that all of us must examine our way of living in light of the needs of the poor. Christian faith and the norms of justice impose distinct limits on what we consume and how we view material goods. The great wealth of the United States can easily blind us to the poverty that exists in this nation and the destitution of hundreds of millions of people in other parts of the world. Americans are challenged today as never before to

develop the inner freedom to resist the temptation constantly to seek more. Only in this way will the nation avoid what Paul VI called "the most evident form of moral underdevelopment," namely greed.[12]

76. These duties call not only for individual charitable giving but also for a more systematic approach by businesses, labor unions, and the many other groups that shape economic life—as well as government. The concentration of privilege that exists today results far more from institutional relationships that distribute power and wealth inequitably than from differences in talent or lack of desire to work. These institutional patterns must be examined and revised if we are to meet the demands of basic justice. For example, a system of taxation based on assessment according to ability to pay[13] is a prime necessity for the fulfillment of these social obligations.

"The Humanitarian—With Hope and Resignation from Darfur"

by Matthew McGarry

It has been more than a year since I stepped off of the plane that brought me to the Sudan to take up a position as area coordinator for Catholic Relief Services in the northernmost sector of West Darfur. Of that, I am certain. Beyond the date of my arrival and a few seminal events, however, the entirety of the last 14 months seems cloaked in an impenetrable haze of the surreal. Why on earth did I come here? Did this last year really happen? What am I still doing here?

I have joked with friends that there are four basic kinds of humanitarian relief workers: those who are here to save the world; those who are here to collect their relief-worker merit badge before taking off for the next danger-ous, exotic destination; those who would rather be anywhere else but can't seem to make it work; and those who have no idea why they are here but continue the work because nothing else makes much sense.

Catholic Relief Services formed in 1943 by the Catholic Bishops of the United States, an international organization that provides immediate aid and promotes long-term development in troubled countries

humanitarian promoting human welfare and social reform

The punch line is that at one time or another we all, myself included, fall into each of these categories. Of course, we are just trying to bring some order to a chaotic existence and would never be so presumptuous as to think that we have any idea of what motivates our colleagues to continue this thankless, frustrating, often futile work.

I do not know how people who have been here for nearly two years manage to maintain an outgoing, upbeat demeanor in the midst of so much madness. I do not know how someone can spend 12 hours a day, seven days a week in a cramped, dirty, 110-degree office with no air conditioning, immersed in human misery, and then pass up the opportunity for a transfer to another posting in a country with candy bars, mixed drinks and an ample coastline. I do not know why anyone else would leave behind home, family and a world that occasionally makes sense in order to come to one of the most godforsaken corners of the earth.

I would not dare to even guess at what lies behind the decisions of the countless inspirational men and women I have met here, but when I ask some of these questions of myself, the only remotely satisfactory answer I can come up with is that I am here because of people like the man I will call Mohamed.

At 33, Mohamed is a gentle, unassuming man from one of Darfur's seminomadic tribes. Trained as a statistician, he has traveled throughout Chad and Sudan, worked as a teacher and acquired functional, halting English. His dreams are modest — a wife, a family, maybe someday a trip to the United States. In spring 2003, he was working in the family business in a small town in the northern part of West Darfur, selling livestock in the market. Then the world came undone.

Mohamed's village was one of the first to be destroyed in the conflict between the Arab militias of Sudan's Islamic regime and the rebel groups composed of members of native African tribes in the Darfur area. His family members and friends were murdered. His modest home, holding all of his earthly possessions, was burnt to the ground. The livestock

Darfur

a province in Western Sudan, in Northeast Africa

Sudan

a country in Northeast Africa, south of Egypt

that constituted his family's job, bank account, social security, health insurance and reason for getting out of bed
in the morning were either slaughtered or stolen. Those
family members who managed to escape on foot were
scattered throughout internally displaced persons camps
in Sudan and refugee camps in Chad.

Ordinarily, this is where Mohamed's story would end.
We would leave him a broken, penniless man, scraping
out a woeful existence in a refugee camp, placing what is
left of his faith and trust in God's mercy and the generosity of the international community. He would be just one
more of the 2 million increasingly forgotten and faceless
Darfuris whose lives have been shattered, perhaps irrevo-
cably, by a violence that is incomprehensible in its feroc-
ity and scope.

Remarkably though, there is more. Somehow Mohamed made it to the capital of the province of West
Darfur, where his English and quiet confidence were sufficient to obtain employment as a food monitor with CRS.
He has become an indispensable leader on a team that
each month distributes vital food assistance to the more
than 110,000 men, women and children affected by the
conflict. Without the work carried out by Mohamed and
other food team members, many of these people would
already have died excruciatingly painful, meaningless
deaths.

Mohamed's job of distributing food requires handing more than tens of thousands of pounds of food to
thousands of tired, hungry and frightened people over the
course of an unbearably hot and dusty day in the middle
of an active war zone. Yet to watch him move among the

desert-hardened men, desperate mothers, wailing children and wasted grandmothers is akin to watching a gifted teacher gain complete control over an unruly classroom. He simply gets things done and, in so doing, makes a significant contribution to staving off a human catastrophe of biblical proportions.

The extent to which humanitarian relief efforts succeed or fail depends in large part on people like Mohamed. Though his official position is food monitor, he is also a translator, logistician, security monitor, community liaison officer, team morale booster, historian, navigator and confidante. Without Mohamed and thousands of other hardworking Sudanese staff, relief operations would grind to a halt, if they ever managed to get started in the first place. If the conflict is ever to reach a peaceful conclusion, it will be largely because of these heroes' tireless efforts on behalf of a community bigger than just their own village or tribe, the traditional boundaries of concern in this intensely tribal society. Their courage and commitment are what make the events of the past several months so tragic.

Darfur Unravels

Last November, the already difficult operating environment in West Darfur began unraveling. As bandits, militias and splinter rebel factions specifically targeted relief organizations, cross-border tensions with Chad increased, large-scale attacks on civilians resumed, and the region slipped into near total anarchy, it became impossible for relief workers to venture out of the relative safety of the province's capital. Those of us still there sit trapped in town, as little as a 30-minute drive from people who desperately need our help.

Nothing I have yet experienced in my life has been as infuriating and heartbreaking as the current situation in West Darfur. All of the gains of the past year — the drops in malnutrition and mortality, the gradual rebuilding of a decimated society, the training that has allowed individuals like Mohamed to flourish — are being erased, and we are utterly powerless to do anything about it. It is one of the peculiar contradictions of life in a conflict zone that those of us who are trying to keep things running day to day have the least control over the macro-level factors that permit us to do our jobs. Paradoxically, the responsibility and privilege of giving a voice to the voiceless millions of Darfur falls largely on those who will never set foot in Darfur nor meet a Darfuri.

Within the next few months, I will be departing West Darfur to assist in the CRS relief and recovery operations in the earthquake-affected areas of Pakistan. But I will first make a stop in the United States to try to reconnect with loved ones, make some sense of the past year and stock up on winter clothing. Though I have been blessed with a loving, supportive family and circle of friends, I already know that I will spend a significant portion of my time at home explaining that no, I am not crazy; that Sudan is in Africa; and, yes, the lives of people I had not met before last year are quite a bit more important to me than my own comfort or quality of life, and they should matter to you as well.

It would be unfair to expect people who are essentially several centuries and an entire world removed from life in Darfur to understand the realities of this isolated patch of desert, but I will try. It is the very minimum that I owe the tens of thousands of men, women and children I have tried to serve while I was here, and who have given me more in return than I would ever have imagined possible. It is the one small thing I can do to repay the immeasurable debt I owe to Mohamed and his team members — my colleagues, my mentors, my friends.

In exchange, these extraordinary men and women have provided me with an example of how to live that I will carry with me for the rest of my days. I can only hope that all of the work will not have been in vain. As they say in Darfur with equal parts hope and resignation, *Insha'alla,* God willing.

For Reflection

1. Write definitions for *commutative justice, distributive justice,* and *social justice*. Provide an example of each.

2. How does the commandment "You shall not steal" apply to larger economic issues such as poverty, health care, and the crisis in Sudan? Explain, citing *Economic Justice for All*.

3. Why is Matthew McGarry involved with Catholic Relief Services? Research Catholic Relief Services and identify four other countries, besides Sudan and Pakistan, where it is working for justice. Identify some of the work CRS is doing in these countries.

4. What are three situations in your community where you see injustice? Explain the situations and identify one thing you can do to address the injustice.

Endnotes

1. Pope Paul VI, *On Evangelization in the Modern World*, 24.

2. *Pastoral Constitution*, 32.

3. Ibid., 25.

4. See para. 39.

5. Josef Pieper, *The Four Cardinal Virtues* (Notre Dame, Ind.: University of Notre Dame Press, 1966), 43–116; David Hollenbach, "Modern Catholic Teachings concerning Justice," in John C. Haughey, ed., *The Faith That Does Justice* (New York: Paulist Press, 1977), 207–231.

6. Jon P. Gunnemann, "Capitalism and Commutative Justice," presented at the 1985 meeting of the Society of Christian Ethics, forthcoming in *The Annual of the Society of Christian Ethics*.

7. *Pastoral Constitution*, 69.

8. Pope Pius XI, *Divini Redemptoris*, 51. See John A. Ryan, *Distributive Justice*, third edition (New York: Macmillan, 1942), 188. The term "social justice" has been used in several different but related ways in the Catholic ethical tradition. See William Ferree, "The Act of Social Justice," *Philosophical Studies*, vol. 72

(Washington, D.C.: The Catholic University of America Press, 1943).

9. *On Human Work*, 6, 9.

10. *Pastoral Constitution*, 29.

11. Ibid. See below, paras. 180–182.

12. Pope Paul VI, On the Development of Peoples (1967), 19.

13. *Mater et Magistra*, 132.

The Eighth Commandment: "You shall not bear false witness against your neighbor."

The eighth commandment forbids misrepresenting the truth in our relations with others. This moral prescription flows from the vocation of the holy people to bear witness to their God who is the truth and wills the truth. (*CCC*, no. 2464)

Introduction

Like the second commandment, the eighth commandment deals broadly with language. In its original context, it served a legal function, requiring honest testimony in settling legal disputes. In the Catholic tradition, its interpretation has broadened to address speech in all life settings and even demand that one live "truthfully." Honesty has come to encapsulate the whole of moral integrity. In our own American tradition, legends such as that of George Washington admitting that he had chopped down the cherry tree or stories about "Honest Abe" Lincoln are told to young children as a way of presenting the value of truth.

Sadly, honesty sometimes appears to be rare in our world today. The examples are numerous. The Enron scandal, which cost unsuspecting investors their savings; the public humiliation of Jayson Blair and the *New York Times* when it was discovered they had misled the public with fabricated stories; and the rampant problem of cheating and plagiarism in schools are but a few of the more recent examples of dishonesty in our society. Can the ancient prohibition against bearing false witness still inspire us today?

An appreciation of the power of language will help us better understand the eighth commandment. In the first chapter of Genesis, God creates by speaking. Human speech has this creative power too. Think about the times you have been praised or encouraged and the way it built up your self-esteem. Unfortunately, language also has the power to destroy. Insults, gossip, and sexist or racist remarks tear down all of us. This is why it is fitting for Bishop Thomas J. Olmsted to teach us that "truth alone is not enough." Separated from love, truth can become a blunt instrument as capable of separating as it is of reconciling.

Our motivation for speaking the truth is just as important as speaking truthfully. Bishop Olmsted addresses the circumstances of truth telling and its connection to speaking with love. To tell the truth out of malice is wrong. Spreading malicious rumors or gossip is obviously contrary to truth; it is a clear-cut example of bearing false witness. We are called to speak with love and share the truth to right wrongs, protect creation, and live the life God calls us to. It is important to note that sharing a truth that might hurt someone is not wrong, if it is shared with love and in the proper circumstance.

James Philipps is a teacher who is concerned with the forms of lying and cheating that work themselves into the lives of his students. He draws particular attention to rumors, gossip, and cheating. Philipps also recognizes the power of language and its ability to affect our relationships. Lying, because it deliberately misleads, separates us from others through distrust and misunderstanding. It can even separate us from God.

Excerpt from *"Jesus Caritas: 'Thou Shalt Not Bear False Witness Against Thy Neighbor'"*

by Bishop Thomas J. Olmsted

Many Kinds of Lies

Lies come in a variety of forms, some of them quite subtle and others quite bold. St. Paul (Eph 4:25) urges us to "put away all falsehood." St. Peter writes (I Pet 2:1), "Rid yourselves of all malice and all deceit, insincerity, envy and all slander." The Catechism

> **caritas**
> Latin word for love; the equivalent of "charity" in English

of the Catholic Church (CCC, 2475ff) lists the following as offenses against truth: false witness and perjury, calumny, flattery, boasting or bragging, and rash judgment.

While these various lies differ significantly, their impact is quite similar. Lies of any shape or form harm other people and sow seeds of distrust in society. They also corrupt the person who lies. Should lying become an ingrained habit, a spiritual vice, the person who lies can reach the point where he no longer is able to distinguish good from bad, right from wrong. His own lies warp his very perception of reality itself. A habitual liar cuts himself off from the truth, and therefore from the source of truth, that is from God; then, he becomes a slave of Satan, the father of lies.

slander, calumny

false and malicious statements intended to damage the reputation of another person

Of course, not all lies are equally serious. As the Catechism of the Catholic Church teaches (2484), *"The gravity of a lie is measured against the nature of the truth it deforms, the circumstances, the intentions of the one who lies, and the harm suffered by its victims."* A common excuse offered in defense of falsehood is the saying, "it was just a little white lie." But, whatever the seriousness may be, every lie is a misuse of the gift of speech. Every lie is a failure in charity and a breach of justice.

Truth Alone Is Not Enough

The gift of speech can be misused, even when we say what is true. While we can speak the truth in love, we can also speak the truth in anger or in jealousy. We can tell the hidden faults of others to persons who have no right to know. When doing so, we injure their reputation and harm their good name, even though we have not lied.

It is good to remember the words of Pope John Paul II about the necessary connection between truth and love. Speaking on the occasion of the canonization of St. Edith Stein, the late Holy Father said that this courageous Jewish convert who was killed by the Nazis at Auschwitz bears witness to something we all need to remember: *"Do not accept anything as the truth if it lacks love. And do not accept anything as love which lacks truth!"*

It is tempting to think that we are free to say whatever we want as long as the facts are true. This temptation seems especially strong when we are standing up for some just cause or opposing something gravely wrong, such as abortion, euthanasia or racial prejudice. How easy it is to slip into ad hominem arguments which amount to an attack on the messenger rather than a rebuttal of the

ad hominem
literally "to the person"; appealing to prejudices by attacking the opponent's character rather than the logic of the opponent's arguments

message. But the Lord asks us to love our enemies, to hate the sin but to love the sinner. Only when we speak the truth in love will the truth build up justice and overcome the injustice that lies have brought about.

Respect for the Truth

While the Eighth Commandment requires that we avoid lies, it also requires us to respect the truth we hear from others. A number of factors can oblige us to refrain from sharing information, factors such as the safety of others, respect for privacy and the right to know. *"No one is bound to reveal the truth to someone who does not have the right to know it."*[1] (CCC, 2489)

A priest, in the Sacrament of Reconciliation, is bound by the strongest sanctions of the Church never to reveal what he has learned while hearing Confessions. Not under any circumstances or pretext may a priest violate what the Church calls the "seal of confession." The Church's Code of Canon Law puts it this way (can. 983), *"The sacramental seal is inviolable; therefore, it is a crime for a confessor in any way to betray a penitent by word or in any other manner or for any reason."*

In addition to the sacred confidentiality required of a priest-confessor, many others in society, such as physicians, lawyers and public officials, are obliged to keep professional secrets. The confidential information that is shared with them must not be handed on to others without a grave and proportionate reason.

Among friends and within families, too, respect for the truth demands an appropriate reserve about what is shared with others. At times, the truth can and should be shared for the sake of the common good. But at other times, respect for privacy is the more loving thing to do and what is more in keeping with justice.

The Splendor of Truth

Why did John Paul II title his famous encyclical on Moral Theology "The Splendor of Truth"? Without a doubt, he was eager to show the close connection between truth and goodness, and between truth and beauty. The Catechism explains (CCC, 2500): *"The practice of goodness is accompanied by spontaneous spiritual joy and moral beauty. Likewise, truth carries with it the joy and splendor of spiritual beauty. Truth is beautiful in itself. . . . But truth can also find other complementary forms of human expression, above all when it is a matter of evoking what is beyond words: the depths of the human heart, the exaltations of the soul, the mystery of God."*

The Eighth Commandment holds a special place in our lives because truth has such a pivotal role in the mission of evangelization. Christ's call to bear witness to the Kingdom of God is a call to speak the truth in love, especially the truth of the Gospel. Those who bear false witness erode the fabric of trust among people and thereby do great harm to the common good. But those who bear witness to the truth contribute to the common good; and those who bear witness to the truth about Christ and His Gospel will shine like the stars for all eternity.

The cost of always telling the truth and living the truth is not insignificant. As Saint Faustina wrote in her famous diary, *"Truth wears a crown of thorns."* But precisely because it unites us with Christ in His sufferings, it also unites us with Him in

> **St. Faustina**
> twentieth-century Polish nun and mystic famous for the diary she kept

his victorious Resurrection. Truthfulness has its own reward that far surpasses the cost it requires. Christ, whom St. Catherine of Siena called *"Gentle Truth,"* more than rewards our truthfulness with His friendship, and with His lasting peace and joy.

"What's Wrong with Lying and Cheating?"

by James Philipps

I remember the night clearly. Only a month or so into my freshman year in the fall of 1976, I was going to my first high school party. My mother reluctantly agreed to let me go, provided that my father would drop me off and pick me up.

After the party had been going on for a while, someone managed to smuggle in a case of beer and share it with us, even though most of us were under the drinking age. Several kids drank too much.

The next morning my father, who hadn't said anything during the ride home, asked me if there was beer at the party.

"Yes," I said.

"Did you have any?" asked my dad.

"No," I lied.

I still feel a sense of guilt and regret.

What Problem?

When I consider why I feel bad about an incident that occurred years ago, my thoughts take me to the heart of what's wrong with lying and cheating. They are words and acts of deception that separate us from the people we love and from the person each of us knows he or she is really meant to be.

A basic definition of lying, according to the *Catechism of the Catholic Church*, is "speaking falsehood with the intention of deceiving"[2] (2482). While it's true that all lies aren't equally as serious—lying about drinking beer one time to my father, for example, is not nearly as serious as lying under oath in a courtroom—all lies are *lies*. And while Christian moral teaching recognizes these distinctions—referred to as the "gravity" (seriousness) of a lie—the conclusion is that, "By its very nature, lying is to be condemned" (*Catechism*, 2485).

There's also a second type of lying. When you hold back information that you know is necessary for another person to get a true picture of the situation, you are also intentionally deceiving. A wonderful Gospel story that I'll talk about shortly gives a clear example of this type of lie.

Cheating is a combination of lying and stealing. When you cheat, you are misleading others in one way or another, and that's lying. Often, cheating also involves taking information or ideas that really belong to someone else.

For example, if you copy from the test on the desk of the really smart student who sits right in front of you and then hand in those answers as your own, you are stealing the results of that student's hard work and study. You are also giving your teacher the false impression that you figured out the answers yourself.

Nobody likes a "spitball" pitcher. That's a player who throws a baseball from the pitcher's mound that's been altered just slightly—either by placing a small amount of saliva or gel on the ball or even by roughing up the surface a bit, perhaps with a small nail file concealed in the pitcher's glove. As a result, the ball moves in unpredictable ways (even the pitcher won't know) and it makes it that much harder for the batter to hit it.

The major leagues don't allow this pitch because it's not the skill of the pitcher that makes the ball harder to hit, yet that's the impression everyone who watches the game gets. In other words, it's cheating.

Perjury, Gossip and Rumors

The Bible has a lot to say about these two issues. The first and clearest prohibitions against lying and cheating with which most Christians are familiar appear in the Book of Exodus.

The Ten Commandments (Exodus 20:1–17) prohibit lying and cheating specifically in the Eighth Commandment, which says, "You shall not bear false witness against your neighbor," and also in the Seventh Commandment, "You shall not steal." (Remember that cheating is a form of stealing.) Let's take a brief look at this idea of "bearing false witness" before we go any further.

perjury
lying while under oath

In ancient times, before there were formal court systems to hear complaints and dispense justice, most disputes were dealt with more informally within a certain tribe or clan (a very extended family).

The only reliable and recognized evidence to determine the guilt or innocence of anyone accused of a crime was the testimony of two or three witnesses asked to stand up at the clan meeting and describe what happened. If those witnesses lied, an innocent life was at stake.

Today, this aspect of "bearing false witness" still survives in our criminal justice system. It's called perjury, and it happens when a witness in a criminal case lies after taking an oath to tell the truth. But I think you will be much more familiar with other types of false witness: gossip and rumors.

Have you ever heard a really "juicy" story about someone at school, something really bad about that person, and just couldn't wait to tell someone else?

If you gave in to this desire (and if you didn't, by the way, you are on the way to a level of maturity that a lot of adults never reach), ask yourself a couple of questions.

Did you stop to check whether or not the rumor was true? Did you ask the subject of the rumor what he or she thought about it? If you didn't, you've learned a lesson about how easy it is to fall into the trap of bearing false witness.

If we look at some of the other books of the Hebrew Bible we find more powerful thoughts on the subject of lying. For example, take Proverbs 19:22: "From a person's greed comes [his or her] shame; rather be poor than a liar."

The biblical books of the prophets, those holy men and women living during the time before Jesus who took the teachings of the Jewish religion very seriously (especially the Ten Commandments), often talk about cheating.

The prophet Amos really tears into the wealthy people of his time who were cheating the poor—the worst kind of cheating imaginable—by overcharging them for the basic necessities of life (Amos 8).

Amos's charge may speak more powerfully to us than to the people of his own time. Every time you put on a pair of sneakers or wear a shirt or buy a coat or bag manufactured in a third-world country, you might unknowingly be involved in a system that regularly cheats the poor.

In some cases these products are being manufactured in so-called "sweatshops" in less economically developed countries where workers make barely enough money to feed and clothe themselves and work in dangerous conditions for over 12 hours a day every day. Our low-priced goods are a result of the unfair wages and inhuman conditions they suffer.

Can't Fool Jesus

It's not surprising that Jesus also understood how important it is to be honest. He was Jewish and therefore knew the value of all of these counsels from his people's Scriptures. But Jesus put his own spin on things—clarifying and simplifying, mostly by using parables and short sayings of his own to get people thinking.

Jesus reminds us, for example, "Let your 'Yes' mean 'Yes,' and your 'No' mean 'No'" (Matthew 5:37). Then there's the parable where Jesus asks us to compare two sons (Matthew 21:28–31). The first son tells his father that he will not do his assigned chores, but later he is sorry and does them. The second son eagerly says he will do them but never really has any intention of following through.

While neither son is perfect, Jesus makes it clear in this story that a response which is basically faithful and honest is much more meaningful than even the sweetest and smoothest lie.

And now let's take a look at the story from John's Gospel I mentioned earlier. It takes place in an out-of-the-way area of the Holy Land known as Samaria and clearly shows an example of withholding information a person needs to get a true picture of the situation.

Samaritans and Jews were related, but they disliked one another. When Jesus speaks to the Samaritan woman who is coming to the center of town to draw water from the well, she is shocked. Nevertheless, she begins chatting with Jesus, not saying much at first but gradually getting more and more comfortable.

> **Samaritans**
> Jews who lived in the region of Samaria and did not worship at the Temple in Jerusalem. Samaritans were looked down upon and discriminated against by Jews of the southern kingdom.

Then Jesus asks what seems to be a simple question, "Do you have a husband?" The woman says, "No," and leaves it at that. There's not much point withholding the truth from God, though.

Jesus says to her (and I always picture him smiling as he says it) that yes, it's true, she has no husband. Actually, she has had *five*, and she's not married to the man she is presently living with! The woman is probably left speechless and awfully embarrassed.

But then something amazing happens. Now that the woman has been stripped of the lie that had previously separated her from Jesus and all he had to give her, she can begin to see him for who he really is. By the story's end, she has become Jesus' first missionary to the people of Samaria (John 4:4–42).

A Lonely Life-style

This story can help us begin thinking about just why lying and cheating are so wrong. Let's go back to where we started—the idea of separation. Every time you lie or cheat, you are choosing to put a little distance between yourself and other people, your true destiny and, ultimately, God.

From time to time, I ask my students what qualities contribute to a good and lasting friendship. One of the first qualities every class comes up with is trust, and that makes a lot of sense.

We all experience a certain amount of difficulty in opening up to and getting close to people we don't know.

We're afraid they won't like us or that they'll make fun of us or will try to trick us.

It takes a great deal of time and experience before we'll trust someone enough to consider him or her a true friend. All it takes is just one lie to set that whole process back or to destroy the friendship altogether.

When I was in the fifth grade, I became friends with a boy whom no one really liked because he was "different." One day, a group of kids came over to me and asked if I was this boy's friend.

I didn't want to seem weird and risk being unpopular, so I lied and said that not only was he not my friend, I didn't even like him. I can still remember how hurt he looked when he found out what I had said.

The effects of lying and cheating go way beyond ourselves, however. Every individual act of lying and cheating contributes to a feeling we all have at times that we just can't trust anyone.

The level of trust in our society has been noticeably affected by too many acts of lying and cheating. We lock up our valuables, keep our guard up against strangers and sometimes give in to the temptations and pressures to lie and cheat because we think "everyone else is doing it."

There's nothing wrong with being cautious, but did you ever stop to think about how many good friendships never happen because of the mistaken belief that no one can be trusted?

Here's something else to think about: If God is absolute truth, wouldn't it follow that the more a person gets used to lying and cheating, the harder it gets to recognize God's presence in his or her life?

All Is Not Lost

The good news is that none of this is inevitable. If we can choose to lie and cheat, then we can also choose to be honest. Think of it this way: Every time you make a decision to be honest when you could have been dishonest, the *world* becomes a little bit more honest. Imagine what could happen if every person made that decision!

If you've fallen into the bad habit of not being truthful, that doesn't mean you have to continue to lie and cheat. Being truthful is a *decision*; it's recognizing, with God's help and the strength that comes through prayer, that the long-term rewards and the rich friendships that come with being a person of integrity are much more valuable than anything you seem to gain in the short term from being dishonest.

Just like acts of dishonesty, honest acts build on one another; the more honest you are, the easier it is to be honest, and the more you'll find yourself surrounded by honest people.

So the next time you feel pressured or tempted to lie or cheat, stop and think for a minute. Try to figure out why you want to be dishonest. Is it out of fear? Anger? A desire to have something that doesn't belong to you? (That's called "coveting" in the Bible.)

Next, think about all that will happen, both in the long and the short term, if you choose the honest response. It won't take long for you to see that the reason you are an honest person is not because you're a "nerd," but because you've made the choice for a life of meaning and meaningful relationships.

For Reflection

1. Why, according to Bishop Olmsted, is being truthful so important? What harm can telling a lie about someone do to that person? What harm can telling a lie do to the person telling it? Explain.

2. What does Bishop Olmsted mean when he says, "Only when we speak the truth in love will the truth build up justice and overcome the injustice that lies have brought about"? What does it mean to speak the truth in love? Write a paragraph explaining these two questions.

3. What responsibility do we have as Christians to not be involved in spreading rumors or gossip? Where in our society do you see rumors and gossip being accepted?

4. How is cheating a form of lying? How does gossiping go against the eighth commandment? Describe a time when you were tempted to cheat or gossip. Why were you tempted? What would you gain from cheating or gossiping? What were the risks? Explain.

Endnotes

1. Cf. *Sir* 27:16; *Prov* 25:9–10.

2. St. Augustine, *De mendacio* 4, 5: J. P. Migne, ed., Patrologia Latina (Paris: 1841–1855) 40, 491.

The Ninth Commandment: "You shall not covet your neighbor's wife."

> St. John distinguishes three kinds of covetousness or concupiscence: lust of the flesh, lust of the eyes, and pride of life.[1] In the Catholic catechetical tradition, the ninth commandment forbids carnal concupiscence; the tenth forbids coveting another's goods. (*CCC*, no. 2514)

Introduction

While previous commandments have addressed external acts, the final two regulate internal dispositions. Inclinations are important because they shape our way of seeing and acting. Thus, it is necessary to develop the ability to desire the right things to an appropriate degree. Though the tenth commandment is concerned with the disposition toward external goods and property, the ninth is particularly focused on overcoming lust and acquiring purity of heart.

The first thing to notice is that the commandment does not imply there is anything sinful about women or sex. They are both created good by God. It does not matter whether the desirable person in question is a woman or a man, whether she or he is married or single, or whether she or he lives next door or is in the movies. In his general audience of October 8, 1980, Pope John Paul II emphasizes that the issue at stake is the way human beings look at one another. He compares two different habitual ways of regarding other human beings. "Lust of the eyes" gazes upon people as objects to be used for one's own satisfaction; "purity of heart" sees others as unique human beings with inherent value. Purity of heart recognizes the dignity of both people and is open to the mutual self-giving of a truly loving relationship. It is important to note that as a young person develops, it is natural to have sexual feelings. What John Paul II is warning against is the fueling of lustful feelings and viewing people as merely objects for sexual gratification.

Christopher West is concerned with two sources of confusion about the human body. The first is a misguided belief that the human body is sinful or the source of sin. The second is that, as a culture, we underestimate the harm abuses of sexuality can do to the God-given gifts of our body and soul. West argues that John Paul II's "theology of the body" can correct this confusion and provide a proper appreciation of the good of the body and sexuality.

Both John Paul II and Christopher West envision a transformed appreciation of the body. There can be no doubt that this is needed. Pornography is an obvious instance of the way the lust of the eyes can distort the good and objectify the beautiful, but it is not the only one. Another example is the way cultural standards of beauty have pushed exercise and diet beyond healthy means and driven many to eating disorders. If the lust of the eyes can be overcome, so can any sense of shame that might otherwise surround the body. Purity of heart can make it possible to see anew the good and the beauty of the body without "objectifying" it.

Interpreting the Concept of Concupiscence

by Pope John Paul II

1. Today I wish to conclude the analysis of the words spoken by Christ in the Sermon on the Mount about adultery and lust, and especially the last element of this enunciation, in which "lust of the eyes" is defined specifically as "adultery committed in the heart."

> **enunciation**
> a systematic declaration

We have already seen that the above-mentioned words are usually understood as desire for another's wife (that is, according to the spirit of the ninth commandment of the Decalogue). However, it seems that this interpretation—a more restrictive one—can and must be widened in the light of the total context. The moral evaluation of lust (of looking lustfully), which Christ called adultery committed in the heart, seems to depend above all on the personal dignity itself of man and of woman. This holds true both for those who are not united in marriage, and—perhaps even more—for those who are husband and wife.

Need to Amplify

2. The analysis which we have made so far of Matthew 5:27–28 indicates the necessity of amplifying and above all deepening the interpretation presented previously, with regard to the ethical meaning that this enunciation contains. "You have heard that it was said, 'You shall not commit adultery.' But I say to you that everyone who looks at a woman lustfully has already committed adultery with her in his heart." Let us dwell on the situation described by the Master, a situation in which the one who commits adultery in his heart by means of an interior act of lust (expressed by the look) is the man. It is significant that in speaking of the object of this act, Christ did not stress that it is "another man's wife," or a woman who is not his own wife, but says generically, a woman. Adultery committed in the heart is not circumscribed in the limits of the interpersonal relationship which make it possible to determine adultery committed in the body. It is not these

> **circumscribed**
> bound or restricted as if enclosed by a line or walls

limits that decide exclusively and essentially about adultery committed in the heart, but the very nature of lust. It is expressed in this case by a look, that is, by the fact that that man—of whom Christ speaks, for the sake of example—looks lustfully. Adultery in the heart is committed not only *because* man looks in this way at a woman who is not his wife, but *precisely* because he looks at a woman in this way. Even if he looked in this way at the woman who is his wife, he could likewise commit adultery in his heart.

To Satisfy His Own Instinct

3. This interpretation seems to take into consideration more amply what has been said about lust in these analyses as a whole, and primarily about the lust of the flesh as a permanent element of man's sinfulness (*status naturae lapsae*). The lust which, as an interior act, springs from this basis (as we tried to indicate in the preceding analyses) changes the very intentionality of the woman's existence "for" man. It reduces the riches of the perennial call to the communion of persons, the riches of the deep attractiveness of masculinity and femininity, to mere satisfaction of the sexual need of the body (the concept of "instinct" seems to be linked more closely with this). As a result of this reduction, the person (in this case, the woman) becomes for the other person (the man) mainly the object of the potential satisfaction of his own sexual need. In this way, that mutual "for" is distorted, losing its character of communion of persons in favor of the utilitarian function. A man who looks in this way, as Matthew 5:27–28 indicates, uses the woman, her femininity, to satisfy his own instinct. Although he does not do so with an exterior act, he has already assumed this attitude deep down, inwardly deciding in this way with regard to a given woman. This

is what adultery committed in the heart consists of. Man can commit this adultery in the heart also with regard to his own wife, if he treats her only as an object to satisfy instinct.

Better Interpretation

4. It is not possible to arrive at the second interpretation of Matthew 5:27–28, if we confine ourselves to the purely psychological interpretation of lust without taking into account what constitutes its specific theological character, that is, the organic relationship between lust (as an act) and the lust of the flesh as a permanent disposition derived from man's sinfulness. The purely psychological (or "sexological") interpretation of lust does not seem to constitute a sufficient basis to understand the text of the Sermon on the Mount in question. On the other hand, if we refer to the theological interpretation—without underestimating what remains unchangeable in the first interpretation (the psychological one)—the second interpretation (the theological one) appears to us as more complete. Thanks to it, the ethical meaning of the key enunciation of the Sermon on the Mount, to which we owe the adequate dimension of the ethos of the Gospel, becomes clearer.

> **Sermon on the Mount**
> Jesus's ethical speech containing the Beatitudes, found in Matthew 5–7

Fulfillment in the Heart

5. Sketching this dimension, Christ remains faithful to the law: "Do not think that I have come to abolish the law and the prophets; I have come not to abolish them but to fulfill them" (Mt 5:17). Consequently he shows how deep down it is necessary to go, how the recesses of the human heart must be thoroughly revealed, in order that this heart may become a place of "fulfillment" of the law. The enunciation of Matthew 5:27–28, which makes manifest the interior perspective of adultery committed in the heart—and in this perspective points out the right ways to fulfill the commandment: "Do not commit adultery"—is an extraordinary argument of it. This enunciation (Mt 5:27–28) refers, in fact, to the sphere which especially concerns purity of heart (cf. Mt 5:8) (an expression which—as is known—has a wide meaning in the Bible). Elsewhere, too, we will consider in what way the commandment "Do not commit adultery"—which, as regards the way in which it is expressed and the content, is a univocal and severe prohibition (like the commandment, "You shall not covet your neighbor's wife," Ex 20:17)—is carried out precisely by means of purity of heart. The severity and strength of the prohibition are testified to directly by the following words of the Sermon on the Mount, in which Christ spoke figuratively of "plucking out one's eye" and "cutting off one's hand," if these members were the cause of sin (cf. Mt 5:29–30). We have already seen that the

> **univocal**
> having one consistent meaning

legislation of the Old Testament, though abounding in severe punishments, did not contribute to "fulfill the law," because its casuistry was marked by many compromises with the lust of the flesh. On the contrary, Christ taught that the commandment is carried out through purity of heart. This is not given to man except at the cost of firmness with regard to everything that springs from the lust of the flesh. Whoever is able to demand consistently from his heart and from his body, acquires purity of heart.

casuistry
the application of general principles to particular cases; also a disparaging term for the tendency to rationalize ethically dubious behavior

Two Become One Flesh

6. The commandment "Do not commit adultery" finds its rightful motivation in the indissolubility of marriage. In it, man and woman, by virtue of the original plan of the Creator, unite in such a way that "the two become one flesh" (cf. Gn 2:24). By its essence, adultery conflicts with this unity, in the sense in which this unity corresponds to the dignity of persons. Christ not only confirms this essential ethical meaning of the commandment, but aims at strengthening it in the depth of the human person. The new dimension of *ethos* is always connected with the revelation of that depth,

ethos
the general outlook, character, or moral values of a person or group

which is called "heart," and with its liberation from lust. This is in order that man, male and female, in all the interior truth of the mutual "for," may shine forth more fully in that heart. Freed from the constraint and from the impairment of the spirit that the lust of the flesh brings with it, the human being, male and female, finds himself mutually in the freedom of the gift. This gift is the condition of all life together in truth, and, in particular, in the freedom of mutual giving. Both husband and wife must form the sacramental unity willed, as Genesis 2:24 says, by the Creator himself.

Mutual Relationship

7. As is plain, the necessity which, in the Sermon on the Mount, Christ placed on all his actual and potential listeners, belongs to the interior space in which man— precisely the one who is listening to him—must perceive anew the lost fullness of his humanity, and want to regain it. That fullness in the mutual relationship of persons, of the man and of the woman, was claimed by the Master in Matthew 5:27–28. He had in mind above all the indissolubility of marriage, but also every other form of the common life of men and women, that common life which constitutes the pure and simple fabric of existence. By its nature, human life is "coeducative." Its dignity and balance depend, at every moment of history and at every

> **coeducative**
> mutually educating both parties

point of geographical longitude and latitude, on who she will be for him, and he for her.

The words spoken by Christ in the Sermon on the Mount have certainly this universal and at the same time profound significance. Only in this way can they be understood in the mouth of him who knew thoroughly "what was in man," and who, at the same time, bore within him the mystery of the "redemption of the body," as St. Paul puts it. Are we to fear the severity of these words, or rather have confidence in their salvific content, in their power?

In any case, the analysis carried out of the words spoken by Christ in the Sermon on the Mount opens the way to further indispensable reflections in order to reach full awareness of historical man, and above all of modern man: of his conscience and he for her.

Excerpt from *"Theology of the Body: A Compelling, Bold, Biblical Response to the Sexual Revolution"*

by Christopher West

"'For this reason a man will leave his father and mother and be united to his wife, and the two will become one flesh.' This is a great mystery, and it refers to Christ and the church" (Eph 5:31–32). . . .

What Makes the Body "Theological"?

To many Christians the phrase "theology of the body" sounds like an oxymoron. Yet such a reaction only demonstrates how far many of us have drifted from an authentic Christian world-view. As John Paul II observed, "Through the fact that the Word of God became flesh the body entered theology . . . through the main door." Because of the Incarnation, the Apostle John can proclaim it is that "which we have touched with our hands" that we proclaim to you concerning the Word of life. And that life was made visible (see 1 Jn 1–3).

We cannot see God; he is pure spirit. But the astounding claim of Christianity is that the invisible God has made himself visible through the human body. For in Christ "the whole fullness of deity dwells bodily" (Col 2:9). God's mystery revealed in human flesh—theology of the body [TOB]: this phrase is not only the title of John Paul II's talks. It represents the very "logic" of Christianity.

Image of God

The Pope's thesis statement proclaims that "only the body is capable of making visible what is invisible: the spiritual and the divine. It has been created to transfer into the visible reality of the world, the mystery hidden from eternity in God, and thus to be a sign of it." This "mystery hidden in God" refers to the eternal union of the three Persons of the Trinity and our privileged invitation in Christ to share in the Trinity's eternal exchange of love. This is the "theology" that the human body signifies.

How? Precisely through the beauty of sexual difference and union. In the normal course of events, the union of the "two" leads to a "third." Here, in a way, we see a trinitarian image. Thus, John Paul concludes that we image God not only as individuals, but also through the union of man and woman. Of course, none of this means that God is "sexual." We use spousal love only as an analogy to help us understand something of God's mystery. God's mystery, itself, remains infinitely beyond any human image.

The Bible, itself, uses spousal love more than any other image to help us understand God's plan. It begins in Genesis with the marriage of Adam and Eve and ends in Revelation with the marriage of Christ and the Church. Here we find a key for understanding the whole of Scripture: God's wants to "marry" us—to live with us in an eternal bond of love that the Bible compares to marriage. But there's more! God wants to fill us—or, to go with the analogy—God wants to "impregnate" us, his bride, with his own divine life. This is a very "earthy" way of speaking, but it isn't mere poetry. In Mary we witness a woman who literally conceived divine life in her womb.

What we learn in the TOB is that God wanted this great "marital plan" of union and eternal life to be so plain to the world that he impressed an image of it right in our bodies by creating us male and female and calling us to become "one flesh." If we have difficulty seeing our bodies this way, it's only because we have been blinded by sin and a deceiver who is literally hell-bent on keeping us from recognizing our true dignity.

"In the Beginning"

On this side of the Fall men and women are often blind to the truth about their bodies and plagued in their union with all kinds of tensions and conflicts. John Paul II reminds us of Christ's words that "in the beginning it was not so" (Mt 19:8). And the "good news" is that Christ came into the world to make God's original plan a reality in our lives. With this approach—the Gospel approach—John Paul shifts the discussion about sexual morality from legalism ("How far can I go before I break the law?") to liberty ("What is the truth about sex that sets me free to love?"). The truth that sets us free to love is salvation in Jesus.

In the beginning "nakedness without shame" (Gen 2:25) reveals a very different experience of sexual desire from our own. God created sexual desire as the power to love as he loves. And this is how the first couple experienced it. Nakedness without shame, in fact, is the key, according to the Pope, for understanding God's original plan for human life. It unlocks the intimacy and ecstasy of love that God intended "from the beginning."

The entrance of shame, then, indicates the dawn of lust, of erotic desire cut off from God's love. We cover our bodies in a fallen world not because they're bad, but to protect their inherent goodness from the degradation of lust. Since we know we're made for love, we feel instinctively "threatened" not only by overt lustful behavior, but even by a "lustful look."

Beyond "Sin Management"

Christ's words are severe in this regard. He insists that if we look lustfully at others, we've already committed adultery in our hearts (see Mt 5:28). John Paul asks whether we should fear Christ's words, or rather have confidence in their power to save us. Here, the Pope sets us on the path of an effective sexual redemption. This is perhaps the most important contribution of the entire TOB.

As we allow our lusts to be crucified with Christ (see Gal 5:24) we can progressively rediscover and live God's original plan for sexual desire. We needn't merely cope with our lusts or "manage" our sinful tendencies. Our sexual desires can be effectively transformed through the "redemption of the body" (Ro 8:23). C. S. Lewis offered a grand image of this at the end of *The Great Divorce* when "the lizard of lust" was transformed into a great white stallion.

> **C. S. Lewis**
> author and philosopher who converted to Christianity and wrote defending the reasonableness of religious belief

Of course, on this side of heaven, we'll always be able to recognize a battle in our hearts between love and lust. Only in eternity will the battle cease, as will marriage as we know it. However, when Christ said we will no longer marry in the resurrection (see Mt 22:30), this doesn't mean our longing for

> **icon**
> a religious image meant to focus and direct the attention of worshipers toward God, rather than being worshiped itself as an idol

union will be obliterated. It means it will be fulfilled in the "Marriage of the Lamb" (Rev 19:7). That is the union we truly crave. The union of the sexes here on earth is only an icon that's meant to point us to heaven. When we get there, the icon will give way to the ultimate reality!

In fact, all the sexual confusion in our world and in our own hearts is simply the human desire for heaven gone berserk. The gift of the TOB is that it helps us "unberserk" it. Lust has inverted our rocket engines causing us to crash and burn. The TOB redirects our rocket engines toward the stars.

True and False Prophets

Only in this context does the Christian sexual ethic make sense. Everything the New Testament teaches about sexual morality is an invitation to embrace the original plan of Genesis in order to launch us toward the marriage in the Book of Revelation.

But here's what truly makes the Gospel good news: it doesn't only give us a list of rules to follow. Christ empowers us with his grace to fulfill the law. As we allow grace to work in us, the law no longer feels like a burden imposed from without. It wells up from within. We embrace the biblical teaching on sex not because we "have" to, but because we long to. When we see the riches of the banquet, the dumpster no longer attracts us.

"For this reason a man will leave his father and mother and be united to his wife, and the two will become one flesh" (Gen 2:24). For what reason? To proclaim and participate in the "great mystery" of Christ's ecstatic union with the Church (see Eph 5:31–32). Could there be a more glorious vision of human sexuality than this?

As a proclamation of divine truth, sexual union has a "prophetic language." But, as the Pope maintained, we must carefully distinguish true and false prophets. If it is possible to speak the truth with the body, it is also possible to speak a lie. Marriage vows are the solemn promise a man and a woman make to love each other "in the image of God." In turn, spouses are meant to express this same love with their bodies whenever they become one flesh. In other words, sexual intercourse is meant to be a renewal of wedding vows—where the words of the vows are made flesh.

grace

unmerited assistance that God freely gives to humans so they can respond to God's invitation to love and pursue holiness

Ecumenical Significance

Since the "one flesh" union offers a prophetic reference to Christ and the Church (see Eph 5:31–32), our understanding of sexuality has ramifications for all of theology—for the very way we conceive of Christ and his Church. Thus, it shouldn't surprise us that disputes about the nature

ecumenical

promoting unity and cooperation among the different Christian denominations around the world of marriage are often at the core of historical divisions within Christianity.

Followers of Christ everywhere recognize John Paul II's tireless ecumenical efforts. He publicly repented on behalf of those Catholics whose sins led to division in the first place. He reached out repeatedly to Protestant and Orthodox leaders, even asking them to help Rome "re-envision" the papacy so that it could more effectively serve the needs of all Christians. Yet, when history witnesses the fulfillment of Christ's prayer that "all may be one" (Jn 17:11), it may well recognize the TOB as John Paul II's most important ecumenical contribution.

> **domestic church**
> the notion, which first appeared in *Lumen Gentium* and was later developed by Pope John Paul II in *Familiaris Consortio*, that the family is a microcosm of the Church in the home where people learn to become Christians together

If disputes in Christ's family have led to multiple divorces, the Pope's daring, biblical apologetic for unity in the "domestic church" (the family) can contribute greatly to bringing about unity in the Church at large. It's precisely here, in fact—in the cultural battle for marriage and the family—that committed Christians of varying professions find themselves overcoming their mutual prejudices and standing together.

Alan Medinger, who has served the sexually broken for a quarter century through Regeneration Ministries, observes that "evangelicals have much to offer the Catholic Church. . . . But this is a two way street. . . . Catholics have [much] to offer [us] in the area of teaching and theology regarding the related matters of life, reproduction, and sexuality." He concludes, "At this point in my ministry, I can think of no greater service to render to my fellow evangelicals than to point them to Theology of the Body."

Cultural Renewal

There will be no renewal of the Church and the world without a renewal of marriage and the family. And there will be no renewal of marriage and the family without a return to the full truth of the Christian sexual ethic. This will not happen, however, unless we can find a compelling way to demonstrate to the modern world that the biblical vision of sexuality is not the prudish list of prohibitions it is so often assumed to be, but rather it is the banquet of love we so desperately yearn for.

This is the gift and the promise of John Paul II's TOB. But its riches have barely begun to penetrate the Catholic world, let alone the wider Christian community. Perhaps if Christians everywhere feasted on this biblical banquet, we could save our culture from its repressive heritage and from the pornographic backlash it inspired. . . .

For Reflection

1. The first eight commandments deal with external acts. How much more difficult is it to control internal thoughts? Why is addressing the way we think important to living a moral life? Explain.

2. How is adultery in the heart similar to the physical act of adultery? How can adultery in the heart harm or prevent a mutually giving relationship as presented in chapter 6? Explain.

3. In what ways does our society promote the sacredness of the human body? In what ways does it promote disrespect for the human body? Examine current advertising, television, movies, and music and identify two examples that promote the dignity of the body or relationships and two examples that present a negative depiction of the body or relationships.

Endnotes

1. Cf. *1 Jn* 2:16.

The Tenth Commandment: "You shall not covet your neighbor's house or anything that belongs to your neighbor."

The tenth commandment unfolds and completes the ninth, which is concerned with concupiscence of the flesh. It forbids coveting the goods of another, as the root of theft, robbery, and fraud, which the seventh commandment forbids. "Lust of the eyes" leads to the violence and injustice forbidden by the fifth commandment.[1] . . . The tenth commandment concerns the intentions of the heart; with the ninth, it summarizes all the precepts of the Law. (*CCC*, no. 2534)

Introduction

In the second chapter of this book, John Paul II provided an interpretation of the story of the rich young man (Matthew 19:16–21). In it, Jesus tells the young person to sell all his possessions and give the money to the poor. Throughout the history of the Church, from the mendicant (begging) religious orders to Dorothy Day and the Catholic Worker movement, there is a tradition of adopting voluntary poverty as a way to follow Jesus. The tenth commandment does not forbid ownership of private property nor demand lives of poverty, but it does require that we strive to not let the obtaining of worldly goods dictate our lives.

In his 1967 encyclical *On the Development of Peoples (Populorum Progressio),* Pope Paul VI looks at a world where science and technology are making great strides forward while the economic gap between advanced and developing nations is widening. The question he asks in response is whether our moral development can keep up with our material progress. Paul VI says this would require "a new humanism" to promote "truly human conditions" for all.

The greed addressed by the tenth commandment is an enormous obstacle to the vision of Paul VI. Coveting doesn't lead only to stealing property directly from others. The "desire to amass earthly goods without limit" (*CCC,* no. 2536) results in an unbalanced distribution of the goods of the earth (which God provided to meet the needs of all) and deprives some people of the basic necessities for life. For that reason, it is another form of theft. Participating in a global economy benefits us through all the commodities it produces, but Paul VI says it also makes us obligated to the other members of the human community. We cannot be indifferent to the material well-being of those who help provide the benefits we enjoy.

The problem with greed is not just its impact on others, but also what it does to us. Excessive desire for things can upset our priorities. Who has not wanted an iPod, designer clothes, or some other item to the extent it has become a preoccupation? This kind of craving can distract us from responsibilities at school, home, and work or even our duties to friends and family—let alone our concerns for justice and fairness with regard to strangers far away. The problem is not the thing itself, but the way our desire for it can bring about the small compromises that eventually corrupt our integrity.

The tenth commandment is very challenging for those of us living in a consumer culture beset by rampant materialism and advertising. In response, Tom Beaudoin offers a few practical and manageable suggestions in his essay "Six Ways to Be a Conscientious Catholic Consumer." Like Paul VI, Beaudoin takes the broadest and most inclusive view possible of the human community. No one can be left out when we weigh the consequences of our economic decisions. Therefore, overcoming consumerism is not something one tries alone; it is something we attempt together.

Excerpts from *On the Development of Peoples (Populorum Progressio)*

by Pope Paul VI

Personal Responsibility

15. In God's plan, every man is born to seek self-fulfillment, for every human life is called to some task by God.

At birth a human being possesses certain aptitudes and abilities in germinal form, and these qualities are to be cultivated so that they may bear fruit. By developing these traits through formal education or personal effort, the individual works his way toward the goal set for him by the Creator.

Endowed with intellect and free will, each man is responsible for his self-fulfillment even as he is for his salvation. He is helped, and sometimes hindered, by his teachers and those around him; yet whatever be the outside influences exerted on him, he is the chief architect of his own success or failure. Utilizing only his talent and willpower, each man can grow in humanity, enhance his personal worth, and perfect himself.

Man's Supernatural Destiny

16. Self-development, however, is not left up to man's option. Just as the whole of creation is ordered toward its Creator, so too the rational creature should of his own accord direct his life to God, the first truth and the highest good. Thus human self-fulfillment may be said to sum up our obligations.

Moreover, this harmonious integration of our human nature, carried through by personal effort and responsible activity, is destined for a higher state of perfection. United with the life-giving Christ, man's life is newly enhanced; it acquires a transcendent humanism which surpasses its

transcendent
surpassing material existence in time

nature and bestows new fullness of life. This is the highest goal of human self-fulfillment.

Ties with All Men

17. Each man is also a member of society; hence he belongs to the community of man. It is not just certain individuals but all men who are called to further the development of human society as a whole. Civilizations spring up, flourish and die. As the waves of the sea gradually creep farther and farther in along the shoreline, so the human race inches its way forward through history.

We are the heirs of earlier generations, and we reap benefits from the efforts of our contemporaries; we are under obligation to all men. Therefore we cannot disregard the welfare of those who will come after us to increase the human family. The reality of human solidarity brings us not only benefits but also obligations.

Development in Proper Perspective

18. Man's personal and collective fulfillment could be jeopardized if the proper scale of values were not maintained. The pursuit of life's necessities is quite legitimate; hence we are duty-bound to do the work which enables us to obtain them: "If anyone is unwilling to work, do not let him eat." But the acquisition of worldly goods can lead men to greed, to

avarice
greed; an excessive or even insatiable desire for material wealth

the unrelenting desire for more, to the pursuit of greater personal power. Rich and poor alike—be they individuals, families or nations—can fall prey to avarice and soulstifling materialism.

Latent Dangers

19. Neither individuals nor nations should regard the possession of more and more goods as the ultimate objective. Every kind of progress is a two-edged sword. It is necessary if man is to grow as a human being; yet it can also enslave him, if he comes to regard it as the supreme good and cannot look beyond it. When this happens, men harden their hearts, shut out others from their minds and gather together solely for reasons of self-interest rather than out of friendship; dissension and disunity follow soon after.

Thus the exclusive pursuit of material possessions prevents man's growth as a human being and stands in opposition to his true grandeur. Avarice, in individuals and in nations, is the most obvious form of stultified moral development.

A New Humanism Needed

20. If development calls for an ever-growing number of technical experts, even more necessary still is the deep thought and reflection of wise men in search of a new humanism, one which will enable our contemporaries to enjoy the higher values of love and friendship, of prayer and

contemplation, and thus find themselves. This is what will guarantee man's authentic development—his transition from less than human conditions to truly human ones.

The Scale of Values

21. What are less than human conditions? The material poverty of those who lack the bare necessities of life, and the moral poverty of those who are crushed under the weight of their own self-love; oppressive political structures resulting from the abuse of ownership or the improper exercise of power, from the exploitation of the worker or unjust transactions.

What are truly human conditions? The rise from poverty to the acquisition of life's necessities; the elimination of social ills; broadening the horizons of knowledge; acquiring refinement and culture. From there one can go on to acquire a growing awareness of other people's dignity, a taste for the spirit of poverty, an active interest in the common good, and a desire for peace. Then man can acknowledge the highest values and God Himself, their author and end. Finally and above all, there is faith— God's gift to men of good will—and our loving unity in Christ, who calls all men to share God's life as sons of the living God, the Father of all men.

Issues and Principles

22. In the very first pages of Scripture we read these words: "Fill the earth and subdue it." This teaches us that the whole of creation is for man, that he has been charged

to give it meaning by his intelligent activity, to complete and perfect it by his own efforts and to his own advantage.

Now if the earth truly was created to provide man with the necessities of life and the tools for his own progress, it follows that every man has the right to glean what he needs from the earth. The recent Council reiterated this truth: "God intended the earth and everything in it for the use of all human beings and peoples. Thus, under the leadership of justice and in the company of charity, created goods should flow fairly to all."

All other rights, whatever they may be, including the rights of property and free trade, are to be subordinated to this principle. They should in no way hinder it; in fact, they should actively facilitate its implementation. Redirecting these rights back to their original purpose must be regarded as an important and urgent social duty.

The Use of Private Property

23. "He who has the goods of this world and sees his brother in need and closes his heart to him, how does the love of God abide in him?" Everyone knows that the Fathers of the Church laid down the duty of the rich toward the poor in no uncertain terms. As St. Ambrose put it: "You are not making a gift of what is yours to the poor man, but you are giving him back what is

St. Ambrose
influential fourth-century bishop of Milan, who was instrumental in bringing about Augustine's conversion

his. You have been appropri-
ating things that are meant
to be for the common use of
everyone. The earth belongs
to everyone, not to the rich."
These words indicate that the
right to private property is not
absolute and unconditional.

No one may appropriate surplus goods solely for his
own private use when others lack the bare necessities
of life. In short, "as the Fathers of the Church and other
eminent theologians tell us, the right of private property
may never be exercised to the detriment of the common
good." When "private gain and basic community needs
conflict with one another," it is for the public authori-
ties "to seek a solution to these questions, with the active
involvement of individual citizens and social groups."

The Common Good

24. If certain landed estates impede the general prosper-
ity because they are extensive, unused or poorly used, or
because they bring hardship to peoples or are detrimental
to the interests of the country, the common good sometimes demands their expropriation.

Vatican II affirms this emphatically. At the same time
it clearly teaches that income thus derived is not for man's
capricious use, and that the exclusive pursuit of personal
gain is prohibited. Consequently, it is not permissible for
citizens who have garnered sizeable income from the
resources and activities of their own nation to deposit a

large portion of their income in foreign countries for the sake of their own private gain alone, taking no account of their country's interests; in doing this, they clearly wrong their country. . . .

> **capricious**
> impulsive or erratic; subject to a change of mind on a whim

A National Duty

48. The duty of promoting human solidarity also falls upon the shoulders of nations: "It is a very important duty of the advanced nations to help the developing nations . . ." This conciliar teaching must be implemented. While it is proper that a nation be the first to enjoy the God-given fruits of its own labor, no nation may dare to hoard its riches for its own use alone. Each and every nation must produce more and better goods and products, so that all its citizens may live truly human lives and so that it may contribute to the common development of the human race.

> **conciliar**
> pertaining to an ecumenical council of the Church, in this case the Second Vatican Council, *Pastoral Constitution on the Church in the Modern World (Gaudium et Spes)*

> **indigence**
> extreme poverty or destitution, wholly lacking any of the comforts of life

Considering the mounting indigence of less developed countries, it is only fitting that a prosperous nation set aside some of the goods it has produced in order to alleviate their needs; and that it train educators, engineers, technicians and scholars who will contribute their knowledge and their skill to these less fortunate countries.

Superfluous Wealth

49. We must repeat that the superfluous goods of wealthier nations ought to be placed at the disposal of poorer nations. The rule, by virtue of which in times past those nearest us were to be helped in time of need, applies today to all the needy throughout the world. And the prospering peoples will be the first to benefit from this. Continuing avarice on their part will arouse the judgment of God and the wrath of the poor, with consequences no one can foresee. If prosperous nations continue to be jealous of their own advantage alone, they will jeopardize their highest values, sacrificing the pursuit of excellence to the acquisition of possessions. We might well apply to them the parable of the rich man. His fields yielded an abundant harvest and he did not know where to store it: "But God said to him, 'Fool, this very night your soul will be demanded from you . . .'"

Six Ways to Be a Conscientious Catholic Consumer

by Tom Beaudoin

"I'm gonna have to check on that."

Lite jazz, then "Mail room, this is Jimmy."

"Um," I stalled, conjuring his face from the Midwestern twang of his greeting. He had a mullet and cranked the Allman Brothers and was one of the few people on earth to whom you would unreservedly loan money or confess besetting sins.

"Hello," he semi-drawled, radio in the background. "OK," I continued. "I bought a belt from your company a while back, and I'm just trying to find out where it was made, who made it, that kind of stuff. Somehow I got transferred from a vice president to you in the mail room."

"Can't help you with that one. Sorry," he said, and I wondered if he wondered how normal this conversation was.

This was phone call number six out of an eventual 43 calls to the headquarters of major corporations. The interrogation became like the ritual in Monty Python's Holy Grail: "What is your name?" "What is your quest?"

I often tried to mumble something about being concerned, as a person of faith, about human dignity. But having been out-pioused by conservatives and out-justiced by liberals too many times in my life, I gave even that meager statement with hesitant self-consciousness. Many young adults like me live with the feeling that

> **branding**
>
> the business practice of creating name recognition and a reputation for quality and desirability

someone somewhere may be suffering because of the way that their coffee, shoes, clothes, or computers are produced, but many are too busy, tired, or already have enough of their own issues to even begin doing anything about it. I was one of them.

Much of the problem lies in the fact that corporate branding—those labels, insignias, and logos of which we are so conscious—influences young adult self-identity to such a deep degree.

So many of us identify so strongly with the brands of products we like that it almost seems natural for us to do so.

By focusing on branding, companies hope to make their logos into a personality—that is, a lifestyle, an image, an identity, or a set of values. Brands should, in the words of one business report,

> **emote**
>
> to express or portray emotion

"emote a distinctive persona." This persona, it is hoped, will be taken on with verve by young consumers—whose collective disposable income stretches into the tens of millions of dollars, averaging more than $100 a week per 16-year-old. And growing into adulthood under corporate branding means that, to a remarkable degree, young adults come to know themselves and are known by peers in and through relationships to brands.

Because I am concerned with how faith communities can sponsor attention to branding, I will suggest some practical ways forward, ways that also may be used and adapted by people with no explicit religious affiliation.

There are two routes to a maturing economic spirituality: the direct and the indirect. Directly addressing economic spirituality in ministry seems to have both advantages and disadvantages. On the one hand, direct approaches can emulate the prophets by confronting people with a faith-based imperative to change our economic ways. On the other hand, without concrete, alternative ways of buying products, and sometimes even with them, the direct approach can lapse into a moralizing and self-righteous pseudo-prophetic preaching. Which is why I advocate an indirect approach alongside the direct. This approach aims not to deal with the end result of economics in everyday life but with the patterns of life that occur many steps before any purchases are made and to create the conditions of mind and heart that make such purchases seem necessary. Let's start with the indirect approaches:

1. People can be encouraged to accept the mysterious depth of their human identity, the irreplaceable uniqueness of their own dignity. But human "dignity" and "mystery" can easily ossify into buzzwords. We must continually find evocative ways of describing dignity and mystery. I propose that we ask ourselves what is that undomesticatable region of ourselves that cannot be bought, cannot be branded? What about us cannot be traded away, drugged up, or dieted off? What about ourselves cannot be sold, sweated away, or co-opted by

an advertiser? How would you describe that dimension of yourself, and what might it mean to live from that place in your economic life?

2. Christians in particular can be vigilant about the economic implications of the church's own spiritual practices. We can question the idea that grace is one person's private property. We can doubt the notion that there are purely "Christian" practices that have escaped influencing and being influenced by the economy.

Most prophetically, we can protest the equating of divine blessing with material wealth, with sales of Christian books, or with big attendance figures in ministry. When St. Ignatius began a ministry of Christian education for children, his own brother strongly objected, saying that no one would come. Ignatius said that "one would be enough." His example reminds us not to reduce the justification for ministry to a quantitative measure, subject inordinately to consumer norms.

We can also question how the church imitates the labor-exploiting tendencies of our economy when we underpay and exploit church workers when we have the resources to do otherwise.

We can question the source of some donations to the church. Most Christian churches and organizations practice a "don't ask, don't tell" donation system, without

> **St. Ignatius**
> sixteenth-century Spanish soldier (1491–1556), who was wounded, converted while convalescing, and subsequently founded the Society of Jesus (Jesuits)

questioning how that money was acquired. Was it earned as a result of exploited labor, of morally questionable investments, of tax evasion, or of cheating an employer?

Finally, we can question where ministry resources are produced or manufactured. For example, is the coffee in the ubiquitous church coffee pot grown and harvested according to fair-trade standards?

The goal of ministry here should be to get itself into a position where it can credibly criticize economic practices in the larger economy.

3. We can undertake media fasts. This requires supporting each other in giving up television, the Internet, or some other media technology for a specific amount of time. This aids us spiritually by encouraging a critical distance from them and the brands they advertise, allowing us to check their influence on our imaginations.

ubiquitous
existing everywhere at the same time

solicitude
anxious or earnest concern and attention

Jesus himself often fasted from the media of his day. He did this through moving back and forth regularly between the active and the contemplative life. In scripture, Jesus is often being called out of prayer to take on the world, a rhythm of solitude and solicitude, retreat and return, reflection and re-engagement.

4. The church can reclaim its role as sponsor of the arts. It can complement the consumption of branded products by

providing resources to encourage young people to create and interpret their own cultural products.

I know of one church that constructed a recording studio to be used by any young musician in the city. These young people are not required to take any orthodoxy test, they are simply welcome to create their own forms of culture under the aegis of the church. It is a marvelous example of the church at the service of the world.

Now the direct approaches:

5. We can draw up declarations of spiritual freedom for our culture, for individuals, families, or communities. The following 10 commitments for such declarations can be used to orient retreats, worship, religious education, or prayer.

aegis
protection, control, or guidance

Dignity. We will embody the dignity of all life as our most basic value by nurturing and protecting human life at all stages and honoring the created goodness of animals and nature.

Stewardship. We will live stewardship of life as our fundamental spiritual practice by regularly taking an honest measure of our life resources, offering a portion to the church or the world.

Solidarity. We will allow the impact of our spending on the poorest and most disadvantaged members of society to influence strongly our purchasing habits. We will inquire into the labor practices of companies we patronize and let businesses know, through our words and deeds, that just wages and working conditions for all laborers are nonnegotiable matters to people of faith and good will.

Community. We will share in co-responsibility for our lives and the lives of others by being accountable to at least one community or family for whom we will be actively present.

Balance. We will craft our schedules by striving for a balanced life, moving between the active and contemplative modes of solitude, community, recreation, and work.

Play. Because all good recreation immerses us in the goodness of creation, we will make play a priority, both in the form of playful activities and in our taste for the comic dimension of everyday life.

Literacy. We will prepare ourselves to transform responsibly our cultures and communities by gaining literacy in our traditions and fluency in our histories.

Local culture. We will be creators as well as consumers of culture, supporting local and indigenous popular culture and interpreting all forms of culture through lenses of faith.

Discernment. We will practice ways of being attentive to the presence of God in the world, alive to the absolute uniqueness of our own gifts, and careful to make moral judgments through an informed conscience.

Disattachment. Knowing that there is no lasting spiritual growth without disattachment from material goods, we strive to avoid getting entangled in material goods by avoiding the extremes of overvaluing them and hating them. We will regularly reassess our relationship to our material goods.

6. We can practice discernment about our economic decisions. This discernment begins with asking ourselves, "How am I using my economic resources?" The hard work of answering such a question may only come through taking up a fashion inventory, investigating where each article of clothing you are wearing was manufactured. At each stage, ask: Who did the work? Were living wages paid? Were safe working conditions present? Were unions allowed?

Overall, what supports or threats to human dignity were part of the production of your goods? And once you know, what steps will you take to honor your deepened economic spirituality?

There is an authentic spiritual impulse at the heart of our branding economy. We use brands to do identity work for us, out of a desire to be recognized by others, by a power greater than ourselves; and the desire to recognize and know others, to commune with others under a power greater than ourselves. And in this recognizing and being recognized, we experience that greater power that draws us inward and outward.

And so our brand economy discloses a task for spiritual maturity: knowing and being known by ourselves and others, without being governed by what we buy.

We can't do without "stuff." There is nothing wrong with buying, nothing wrong with the existence of brands. But in order to turn the spiritual corner before us we need to integrate who we are with what we buy.

We live out our relation to our ultimate meaning through what and how we buy. Let the integration of faith and economy be the mark of the true spiritual seeker today, a consuming faith.

For Reflection

1. According to Pope Paul VI, how does the "exclusive pursuit of material possessions" prevent man's growth? Provide specific references to the reading.

2. What do the writings in chapter 9, addressing the seventh commandment, and chapter 12, addressing the tenth commandment, have in common? Provide specific examples of similar issues being addressed.

3. How do name brands and current trends promote coveting goods? Identify three of the current "must-have" items. What were three things that were "must-have" items when you were younger? Are they still important to you?

4. Write up a personal declaration of spiritual freedom using the ten commitments Tom Beaudoin presents

under item 5 in his article. State what each of the items means to you and give an example of what it looks like in your life.

Endnotes

1. Cf. *1 Jn* 2:16; *Mic* 2:2.

Appendix

Additional Reading

Catholics have a wealth of resources to draw on for their ethical deliberations. Our community of shared moral inquiry draws on official Church documents, the works of professional theologians, and the reflections of faithful laypeople. The writings included in this book are but a small sample of the rich and ongoing conversation about the requirements of the Christian moral life. The following list is hardly exhaustive, but it is intended to suggest further reading to assist in the formation of a fully informed conscience. Vatican documents are listed first, followed by publications of the U.S. Catholic bishops, and then other materials, each in reverse chronological order (beginning with the most recent). The Church documents can be found at the Vatican Web site (*www.vatican.va*) or the United States Catholic bishops' Web site (*www.usccb. org*). The books should be readily available at libraries, bookstores, or online retailers.

Moral Theology
Reason Informed by Faith: Foundations of Catholic Morality, Richard M. Gula, Paulist Press, 1998

Common Good, Uncommon Questions: A Primer in Moral Theology, Timothy Backous and William C. Graham, eds., Michael Glazier Books, 1997

Contemporary Christian Morality: Real Questions, Candid Responses, Richard Sparks, Crossroad / Faith and Formation, 1996

Principles for a Catholic Morality, revised edition, Timothy E. O'Connell, HarperSanFrancisco, 1990

The Ten Commandments

The Ten Commandments for Today, Walter J. Harrelson, Westminster John Knox, 2006

Commandments of Compassion, James F. Keenan, Sheed and Ward, 1999

The First Commandment: "I am the LORD your God . . . you shall have no other gods before me."

The Lord Jesus (Dominus Iesus), Congregation for the Doctrine of the Faith, 2000

Economic Justice for All: Pastoral Letter on Catholic Social Teaching and the U.S. Economy, nos. 35–40, United States Conference of Catholic Bishops, 1986

Declaration on Religious Freedom (Dignitatis Humanae), nos. 1–6, Second Vatican Council, 1965

Pastoral Constitution on the Church in the Modern World (Gaudium et Spes), nos. 19–21, Second Vatican Council, 1965

The Second Commandment: "You shall not make wrongful use of the name of the LORD your God."

Redemptoris Missio (Mission of the Redeemer), Pope John Paul II, 1990

The Third Commandment: "Remember the sabbath day, and keep it holy."

The Sacrament of Charity (Sacramentum Caritatis), Pope Benedict XVI, 2007

Dogmatic Constitution on the Church (Lumen Gentium), nos. 11 and 33–34, Second Vatican Council, 1964

The Fourth Commandment: "Honor your father and your mother."

Letter to the Elderly, Pope John Paul II, 1999

Blessings of Age, United States Conference of Catholic Bishops, 1999

The Dignity of Older People and Their Mission in the Church and in the World, Pontifical Council for the Laity, 1998

Letter to Families, no. 15, Pope John Paul II, 1994

The Fifth Commandment: "You shall not murder."

A Culture of Life and the Penalty of Death, United States Conference of Catholic Bishops, 2005

Homily at the Trans World Dome (27 January), Pope John Paul II, 1999

Welcome Ceremony Address in St. Louis (26 January), Pope John Paul II, 1999

Living the Gospel of Life: A Challenge to American Catholics, United States Conference of Catholic Bishops, 1998

Dead Man Walking: An Eyewitness Account of the Death Penalty in the United States, Sr. Helen Prejean, 1994

Respect for Life (Donum Vitae), Congregation for the Doctrine of the Faith, 1987

The Challenge of Peace: God's Promise and Our Response, United States Conference of Catholic Bishops, 1983

A Consistent Ethic of Life: An American-Catholic Dialogue (December 6, Gannon Lecture at Fordham University), Joseph Cardinal Bernardin, 1983

Declaration on Euthanasia, Congregation for the Doctrine of the Faith, 1980

Declaration on Procured Abortion, Congregation for the Doctrine of the Faith, 1974

Peace on Earth (Pacem in Terris), Pope John XXIII, 1963

The Sixth Commandment: "You shall not commit adultery."

Address to Members of the Pontifical John Paul II Institute for Studies on Marriage and Family on the 25th Anniversary of Its Foundation, Pope Benedict XVI, 2006

The Christian Family in the Modern World (Familiaris Consortio), Pope John Paul II, 1981

The Original Unity of Man and Woman, Pope John Paul II, 1979–1980 (This "Catechesis on the Book of Genesis" is a series of papal addresses given each Wednesday during this period.)

Pastoral Constitution on the Church in the Modern World (Gaudium et Spes), nos. 47–52, Second Vatican Council, 1965

The Seventh Commandment: "You shall not steal."

On the One Hundredth Anniversary of Rerum Novarum (Centesimus Annus), nos. 30–43, Pope John Paul II, 1991

On Human Work (Laborem Exercens), nos. 18–19, Pope John Paul II, 1981

On the Development of Peoples (Populorum Progressio), nos. 22–24, Pope Paul VI, 1967

Pastoral Constitution on the Church in the Modern World (Gaudium et Spes), nos. 26, 63–72, Second Vatican Council, 1965

Peace on Earth (Pacem in Terris), nos. 18–22, Pope John XXIII, 1963

On Christianity and Social Progress (Mater et Magistra), nos. 68–81, Pope John XXIII, 1961

The Reconstruction of the Social Order (Quadragesimo Anno), nos. 44–52, 63–75, Pope Pius XI, 1931

On the Condition of Labor (Rerum Novarum), nos. 5–10, 15, 36, Pope Leo XIII, 1891

Summa Theologiae, II-II, Q. 66, Thomas Aquinas

The Eighth Commandment: "You shall not bear false witness against your neighbor."

Lying: Moral Choice in Public and Private Life, Sissela Bok, Vintage, 1999

Secrets: On the Ethics of Concealment and Revelation, Sissela Bok, Vintage, 1989

Declaration on Religious Freedom (Dignitatis Humanae), no. 2, Second Vatican Council, 1965

On the Means of Social Communication (Inter Mirifica), Pope Paul VI, 1963

Summa Theologiae, II-II, Q. 109–110, St. Thomas Aquinas

Against Lying, St. Augustine

On Lying, St. Augustine

The Ninth Commandment: "You shall not covet your neighbor's wife."

Blessed Are the Pure in Heart: A Pastoral Letter on the Dignity of the Human Person and the Dangers of Pornography, Bishop Robert Finn, 2007

Modesty Starts with Purification of the Heart, Bishop John W. Yanta, 2006

Address to the Members of the Religious Alliance against Pornography, Pope John Paul II, 1992

On the Dignity and Vocation of Women (Mulieris Dignitatem), no. 29, Pope John Paul II, 1988

The Lord and Giver of Life (Dominum et Vivificantem), nos. 55–57, Pope John Paul II, 1986

Statement on Prostitution and Pornography, Canadian Conference of Catholic Bishops, 1984

Pastoral Constitution on the Church in the Modern World (Gaudium et Spes), no. 24, Second Vatican Council, 1965

The Tenth Commandment: "You shall not covet your neighbor's house or anything that belongs to your neighbor."

Following Christ in a Consumer Society: The Spirituality of Cultural Resistance, John T. Kavanaugh, Orbis Books, 2006

Loaves and Fishes, chaps. 6 and 8, Dorothy Day, Orbis Books, 1997 (You can find more writing by Dorothy Day about voluntary poverty on the Catholic Worker Web site: *www.catholicworker.org.*)

Mission of the Redeemer (Redemptoris Missio), no. 16, Pope John Paul II, 1990

On Social Concern (Sollicitudo Rei Socialis), nos. 27–30, Pope John Paul II, 1987

Economic Justice for All: Pastoral Letter on Catholic Social Teaching and the U.S. Economy, nos. 48–52, United States Conference of Catholic Bishops, 1986

On Evangelization in the Modern World (Evangelii Nuntiandi), no. 55, Pope Paul VI, 1975

A Call to Action (Octogesima Adveniens), no. 9, Pope Paul VI, 1971

Pastoral Constitution on the Church in the Modern World (Gaudium et Spes), no. 35, Second Vatican Council, 1965

Acknowledgments

The scriptural quotations contained herein are from the New Revised Standard Version of the Bible, Catholic Edition. Copyright © 1993 and 1989 by the Division of Christian Education of the National Council of the Churches of Christ in the United States of America. All rights reserved.

All excerpts in this book marked *Catechism* or *CCC* are from the English translation of the *Catechism of the Catholic Church* for use in the United States of America. Copyright © 1994 by the United States Catholic Conference, Inc.—Libreria Editrice Vaticana. English translation of the *Catechism of the Catholic Church: Modifications from the Editio Typica* copyright © 1997, United States Catholic Conference, Inc.—Libreria Editrice Vaticana.

The adapted quotation on page 9, the excerpt on page 14, and the section titled "Excerpts from *Pastoral Constitution on the Church in the Modern World (Gaudium et Spes)*" on pages 16–22 are from *Pastoral Constitution on the Church in the Modern World (Gaudium et Spes)*, numbers 16, 4, and 12–18, by the Second Vatican Council, at *www.vatican.va/archive/hist_councils/ii_vatican_council/documents/vat-ii_cons_19651207_gaudium-et-spes_en.html*, accessed June 8, 2007.

The section titled "Excerpt from *Moral Wisdom: Lessons and Texts from the Catholic Tradition*" on pages 23–30 is from *Moral Wisdom: Lessons and Texts from the Catholic Tradition*, by James F. Keenan (Lanham, MD: Sheed and Ward, 2004), pages 14–18. Copyright © 2004 by James F. Keenan. Used with permission of Sheed and Ward.

The section titled "Excerpt from *The Splendor of Truth (Veritatis Splendor)*" on pages 34–40 is from the encyclical *The Splendor of Truth (Veritatis Splendor)*, numbers 6–10, by Pope John Paul II, at *www.vatican.va/edocs/ENG0222/_P3.HTM*, accessed June 10, 2007.

The section titled "Excerpts from 'Understanding Sin Today'" on pages 41–51 is from "Understanding Sin Today," by Richard M. Gula, in *Catholic Update*, at *www.americancatholic.org/Newsletters/CU/ac0197.asp*, accessed May 23, 2007. Used with permission of St. Anthony Messenger Press, *www.americancatholic.org*.

The section titled "Excerpts from *God Is Love (Deus Caritas Est)*" on pages 55–62 is from *God Is Love (Deus Caritas Est)*, numbers 1, 9, and 16–18, respectively, by Pope Benedict XVI, at *www.vatican.va/holy_father/benedict_xvi/encyclicals/documents/hf_ben-xvi_enc_20051225_deus-caritas-est_en.html*, accessed June 8, 2007.

The quotation on page 120 and the section titled "Excerpt from *The Gospel of Life (Evangelium Vitae)*" on pages 121–126 are from *The Gospel of Life (Evangelium Vitae)*, numbers 2, 12, and 1–3, respectively, by Pope John Paul II, at *www.vatican.va/edocs/ENG0141/_P1.HTM*, accessed June 10, 2007.

The section titled "Excerpt from *All Quiet on the Western Front*" on pages 126–136 is from *All Quiet on the Western Front*, by Erich Maria Remarque, translated from the German by A. W. Wheen (New York: Little, Brown and Company), pages 183–193. Copyright © 1929, 1930 by Little, Brown and Company; renewed © 1956, 1958 by Erich Maria Remarque. Used with permission of the Estate of Paulette Goddard Remarque.

The quotation by John Paul II on page 138 and the section titled "Excerpt from Letter to Families" on pages 140–147 are from Letter to Families from Pope John Paul II, number 11, at *www.vatican.va/holy_father/ john_paul_ii/letters/documents/hf_jp-ii_let_02021994_families_en.html*, accessed June 10, 2007.

The quotation on page 139 and the section titled "Excerpts from *The Holy Longing: The Search for a Christian Spirituality*" on pages 147–153 are from *The Holy Longing: The Search for a Christian Spirituality*, by Ronald Rolheiser (New York: Doubleday, 1999), pages 196–202. Copyright © 1999 by Ronald Rolheiser. Used with permission of Doubleday, a division of Random House.

The quotation on page 157 and the section titled "Excerpt from *Economic Justice for All: Pastoral Letter on Catholic Social Teaching and the U.S. Economy*" on pages 157–164 are from *Economic Justice for All: Pastoral Letter on Catholic Social Teaching and the U.S. Economy*, numbers 75 and 63–76, by the United States Conference of Catholic Bishops (USCCB) (Washington, DC: USCCB, 1986). Copyright © 1986 by the USCCB. Used with permission of the USCCB. All rights reserved.

The section titled "The Humanitarian—With Hope and Resignation from Darfur," on pages 164–170 is from "The Humanitarian—With Hope and Resignation from Darfur," by Matthew McGarry, at *sudan.crs.org/ ownwords_humanitarian.html*, accessed July 18, 2007. Used with permission of Catholic Relief Services.

The quotation on page 174 and the section titled "Excerpt from 'Jesus Caritas: "Thou Shalt Not Bear False Witness Against Thy Neighbor"'" on pages 175–180 are from "Jesus Caritas: 'Thou Shalt Not Bear False Witness Against Thy Neighbor,'" part 3, by Bishop Thomas J. Olmsted, in *The Catholic Sun Online*, August 17, 2006, at *www.catholicsun.org/ bishop/081706bishop.html*, accessed June 10, 2007. Used with permission of *The Catholic Sun Online*.

The section titled "What's Wrong with Lying and Cheating?" on pages 180–189 is from "What's Wrong with Lying and Cheating?" by James Philipps, in *Youth Update*, at *www.americancatholic.org/Newsletters/YU/au0898.asp*, accessed May 23, 2007. Used with permission of St. Anthony Messenger Press, *www.americancatholic.org*.

The section titled "Interpreting the Concept of Concupiscence" on pages 193–200 is from "Interpreting the Concept of Concupiscence," by Pope John Paul II, in *L'Osservatore Romano, English Edition,* October 13, 1980. Used with permission of Libreria Editrice Vaticana.

The section titled "Excerpt from 'Theology of the Body: A Compelling, Bold, Biblical Response to the Sexual Revolution'" on pages 200–208 is from "Theology of the Body: A Compelling, Bold, Biblical Response to the Sexual Revolution," by Christopher West, at *www.christopherwest.com/article12.asp*, accessed July 4, 2007. Used with permission of Theology of the Body Institute.

The quotations on page 211 and the section titled "Excerpts from *On the Development of Peoples (Populorum Progressio)*" on pages 212–220 are from *On the Development of Peoples (Populorum Progressio)*, numbers 20, 21, 15–24, 48, and 49, respectively, by Pope Paul VI, at *www.vatican.va/holy_father/paul_vi/encyclicals/documents/hf_p-vi_enc_26031967_populorum_en.html*, accessed June 10, 2007.

The section titled "Six Ways to Be a Conscientious Catholic Consumer" on pages 221–229 is from *Consuming Faith: Integrating Who We Are with What We Buy*, by Tom Beaudoin (Lanham, MD: Sheed and Ward, 2003), pages ix–x, 4, 97–104, and 106–107, respectively. Copyright © 2003 by Thomas More Beaudoin. Used with permission of Sheed and Ward.

To view copyright terms and conditions for Internet materials cited here, log on to the home pages for the referenced Web sites.

During this book's preparation, all citations, facts, figures, names, addresses, telephone numbers, Internet URLs, and other pieces of information cited within were verified for accuracy. The authors and Saint Mary's Press staff have made every attempt to reference current and valid sources, but we cannot guarantee the content of any source, and we are not responsible for any changes that may have occurred since our verification. If you find an error in, or have a question or concern about, any of the information or sources listed within, please contact Saint Mary's Press.